T0308844

TITANIC

THE OFFICIAL COOKBOOK

TITANIC

THE OFFICIAL COOKBOOK

40 TIMELESS RECIPES
FOR EVERY OCCASION

VERONICA HINKE

INSIGHT
EDITIONS

SAN RAFAEL • LOS ANGELES • LONDON

CONTENTS

# INTRODUCTION

A great deal is owed to the passengers and crew members on the *Titanic* who carefully tucked dining-room menus into the pockets of their suit coats and uniforms. Thanks to these individuals, we have a record of the meals served on this now legendary ocean liner during its ill-fated voyage across the Atlantic. A few passengers even wrote letters home describing meals and drinks. Each menu and description of the food served on the ship gives us a handful of breadcrumbs that reveal clues about the onboard dining experience and demystify distinct, defining points of a captivating, bygone way of life.

This cookbook features recipes and historical information reflecting the three classes of service on the *Titanic*—first class, second class, and third class—as well as the intriguing array of contrasting cultures that were represented among the ship's passengers.

Pizza—which had only recently been introduced in New York City a few years before the *Titanic* sailed in April 1912—and fried calamari with Scotch Bonnet pepper marinara sauce are tributes to the throngs of Europeans who were immigrating to America in third class. Lamb lollipops with mint jelly and sweet pea pesto, herrings in fresh lemon-thyme sauce, and rich, gooey Guinness Welsh rarebit sliders are modern adaptations of some of the opulent foods served in the first-class dining room. Hominy, curried chicken, and other foods that were served in second class are examples of what meals were like for the working middle class.

Recipes showcase ingredients from all four seasons, providing flexibility for hosting a *Titanic*-themed celebration at any time of year. Although lamb, asparagus, rhubarb, and other spring ingredients were the crown jewels of the *Titanic*'s mid-April Atlantic crossing, baked apples, roasted turkeys, plum puddings, and plenty of other fall and winter foods also had starring roles on the ship's menus.

Several recipes in this cookbook are inspired by the favorite pastime of a trip to the movies. In these pages you'll find whimsical twists on popular movie-theater snacks like cardamom malted milk balls, spicy caramel corn, and raspberry gumdrops.

This volume also includes trivia questions about James Cameron's *Titanic*, the epic 1997 film starring Kate Winslet and Leonardo DiCaprio, and sentimental games such as Old Maid, Tiddlywinks, and The Game of Peter Coddles. These were the Uno, Scrabble, and Twister of their day.

Also included is historical information to help plan your festivities, a pre-Prohibition entertaining checklist, popular quotes from the movie, and quick facts about Edwardian foods, cocktails, and entertaining customs.

The *Titanic* and her story are a time capsule of Edwardian traditions. Her abrupt sinking seems to foreshadow the rapid disintegration, soon afterward, of a steadfast popular culture and style, as well as relentless class divides, that had endured for centuries. The First World War and, later, in the United States, Prohibition, propelled winds of change that forever altered societal norms, customs, and everyday life as it had been known.

Fascination with these dramatic cultural shifts has, in part, fueled fascination with the *Titanic*. Books, music, art, and exhibitions memorializing the great ship continue to have a large popular-culture audience.

Few of these commemorative endeavors have captured hearts like the 1997 coming-of-age romance film *Titanic*. One of the reasons the movie is so successful is because of its respectful portrayal of some of the most inspiring heroes in history.

With this volume as your guide, let your *Titanic*-themed party celebrate the incredible people of the *Titanic* with the same thoughtfulness and purpose as the movie. Take steps to create a fun and memorable gathering, and make it count!

TRADITIONAL EDWARDIAN TABLE SETTINGS

During the time period shortly before the *Titanic* sailed, from 1901 to 1910, Queen Victoria's son, Edward VII, was King of England. Named in his honor, the Edwardian years were peaceful, with economic prosperity for the upper crust. In typical high-society households, both in England and the United States, a happy dinner party or a pleasant afternoon tea was almost always being planned.

THE EDWARDIAN DINNER TABLE

Edwardian table settings were more streamlined than the extravagant tables of the Victorian era—which eponymously marked Queen Victoria's reign from 1837 to 1901—and table decorations were simpler. Candelabras, in various heights and volume, were placed in the center of the tables, and some were topped with small candle shades. Also on the tables were high and low vases that were filled with seasonal flowers. American beauty roses and world beater roses were very popular.

Sets of silverware came in a variety of designs, and in many households, they were kept in a rectangular wooden case designed specifically to store silverware. Hostesses would sometimes even use a tape measure to check the distance between items in table settings to make sure every element of the setting was precisely positioned. Cutlery was arranged so that guests worked inwards, moving to the next piece of silverware with each course.

Three forks were placed to the left of the plate. The fish fork was placed on the outside, the entrée fork was placed in the middle, and the meat fork was placed closest to the service plate. On the right side of the service plate, the fruit fork was placed on the outside, next to the soup spoon, which was next to the fish knife. The meat knife was placed next to the service plate. Glasses were placed above the silverware on the right side. The water glass was placed above the meat knife. The Champagne glass was set directly above the soup spoon, and the sherry glass was set directly below the Champagne glass. A tiny cup for nuts was set above the serving plate.

Dinners could last for hours and include as many as twelve to fourteen courses. In the drawing room before dinner, the first course, hors d'oeuvres, would be served with cocktails. Guests would then be seated in the dining hall, and the second course would begin. Soup was followed by fish—served hot or cold—then an entrée, a roast, salad, and sweets, followed with a fruit and cheese course, with several courses of sorbet served in between. Elegant dinners typically began later in the evening, most often from 8 to 9 p.m. Guests arrived "fashionably early," which was 15 minutes before the time stated on the invitation.

5 ESSENTIAL SERVING ITEMS

SILENCE CLOTH

A flannel cloth known as a silence cloth was placed over the table before the tablecloth was spread out. The cloth was helpful in reducing the rattle of dishes and silverware moving around on the table, and it also helped protect the table, which most often was made of wood. In 1911, lifestyle journalist Edith Barnard Delano suggested that the silence cloth should be made of "specially woven, double-faced Canton flannel—the thicker the better" and that it should be covered "with a pure white cloth of linen damask." Others preferred a knitted silence cloth or a quilted cloth. Some hostesses made their own silence cloth by placing several layers of soft papers between two cheesecloths.

CELERY DISH

Celery was a delicacy for only the wealthiest Edwardians to enjoy. Like crackers or chips at dinner today, celery on the table provided a quick and easily prepared handheld crunchy nibble at dinners. In 1910, you could purchase a cut-glass celery dish, on sale, for $2.50. Celery dishes were narrow, long dishes that held long pieces of celery. They were constructed using a variety of materials, including glass, ceramic, china, and more. Some were beautifully painted, while others were simple and made of clear glass. The earlier version of the flat celery dish was the celery vase, which was a popular item to have on the table during the Victorian era.

A celery dish was one of the prizes at a Catholic Young Women's Club fundraiser event that was held at the Hotel Casey in Scranton, Pennsylvania, in 1913.

In 1913, a few days before Christmas, Walter Clark and Stella Egan got married in the Star of the Sea Church in Long Branch, New Jersey. They received many gifts, including numerous silver items such as a soup ladle, fruit knives, jelly spoons, and a soup tureen. A special painting from Japan was given to them. (As more and more Edwardians began traveling to Japan, Japanese-style household items became increasingly popular, and the style was reflected in everything from dishes to linens and more.) The Clarks also received three celery dishes.

On December 2, 1905, in Chicago, Mr. and Mrs. Josiah Tandy threw a party to celebrate their twentieth wedding anniversary. The popular couple received dozens of fashionable gifts, including celery dishes from each of the four different couples who attended the party. The couple also received multiple berry sets and chocolate sets, which included a chocolate pot and cups.

BERRY SETS

Wealthy Edwardian households had at least one set of pretty berry dishes. A berry set included one large bowl and six smaller matching bowls for serving blueberries, strawberries, raspberries, and other berries. Some sets were made of glass—often colored—and others were made of china, porcelain, or another material. They were often decorated with painted flowers, and some sets included a platter instead of a large service bowl.

CHOCOLATE POTS

Hot chocolate was popular with Edwardians. Chocolate pots, as well as sets of pots and cups, were often given as wedding, anniversary, or shower gifts. In 1911, the price of a chocolate pot ranged from 50 cents to $2.50. They were typically made of French, German, or Japanese china. Some were very ornate, while others were plain.

Shortly before the *Titanic* struck the iceberg, passengers were keeping warm, sipping hot whiskey and hot lemonade (hot water with lemon), hot toddies, and other beverages. Hot chocolate and other steamy drinks were also served aboard the *Titanic*. Silver chocolate pots that looked like tall, large coffee pots were aboard the *Titanic*.

CALLING CARD RECEIVER

A receiving tray, or a dish, full of calling cards in an Edwardian home was similar to today's list of friends in social media circles. Calling card receivers were also popular gifts for weddings and anniversaries. Receivers were placed by the front door, and guests understood that they were expected to leave their card in it. Most receivers were made of silver or metal, and some were a mix of glass and metal. Some receivers stood on pedestals, while tray-style receivers lay flat on a table.

Upper-class Edwardians would drop a calling card at someone's home, expecting that they might receive an invitation to dinner. Calling cards were also dropped to let someone know they were being thought of after a death or birth, an engagement, or another special occasion. Leaving a card was also a way of saying thank you for a dinner, gift, or special favor. Some cards included scenes or photos of the person. There was space on the back where a quick note could be written.

10 DOS & 10 DON'TS FOR EDWARDIAN ENTERTAINING

In the Edwardian era, two sure signs of a well-heeled member of the upper class were their polished manners and mastery of etiquette. An upper-class hostess arranging a dinner party during the Edwardian era would have followed these important guidelines.

DO

- Send invitations four to six weeks in advance of the party. Fill-in-the-blank invitation templates were often used, and they could be purchased at stationery shops. Invite an equal number of men and women. Consider inviting people you would like to get to know better.

- Have topics planned for conversation, and keep guests focused on the topics that you introduce.

- Create a seating arrangement, with the highest-ranking woman seated to the left of the host. Write out each guest's name on a name card and arrange the name cards on the table before the guests arrive.

- Place a calling-card holder in the entryway for guests to place their calling card before going inside.

- When it is time to sit down for dinner, the host takes the highest-ranking lady to the dinner table, and the hostess takes the highest-ranking man to the table.

- The host should motion to each guest to show them their seat, and he should remain standing until all the guests have taken their seats.

- The host and hostess should sit at opposite ends of the table, so that every guest can engage with one of them. The hostess should sit at the head of the table.

- The phrase "keep a stiff upper lip" refers to the rule of restraint. Hold back from showing too much emotion about anything, good or bad.

- The host should signal the end of dinner with a smile or nod to the lady of ranking who is seated next to him. She should be on the lookout for the signal, and rise from the table.

- Guests should leave the dining room in the order in which they entered. Although in the Victorian era it was customary for the women to be served coffee in the drawing room while the men remained at the table to smoke cigars or cigarettes, this tradition became less popular in the Edwardian years.

DON'T

- Shake hands.

- Men should never receive anything ahead of the ladies who are with them. He should make sure she is always accommodated first.

- Men should never leave their hat on in the presence of someone of higher social standing.

- Avoid asking someone a question just before they take a bite of food. Edwardians were very careful not to talk with food in their mouths.

- Never let on if one thing tastes better than another. Try to give even feedback on everything, and do not hint at a favorite item.

- A host should never say anything negative about the other host or criticize or correct the other host in front of guests.

- Resist the urge to thank the serving staff or to make a fuss over how well they are looking after everyone.

- Don't set one dish down in favor of another dish. Take a little of everything.

- Just take a little: No matter how great something tastes, hold back from eating too much of anything.

- Women should never wear gloves during dinner. They should wear them, and leave them on until dinner is served. When dinner is served, they should remove their gloves, place them on their lap, and cover them with their dinner napkin that is in front of them on the table.

PARLOR GAMES & ENTERTAINMENT

Games are a wonderful way to break the ice and create lasting memories with very little effort. Treat guests to an immersive Edwardian experience with games that were popular when the *Titanic* sailed. Dubbed "parlor games," these core games kept partygoers entertained in early twentieth-century parties. Raise the stakes and play these games for *Titanic*-themed prizes such as books, replica *Titanic* serving dishes, or other novelty gifts. Tiddlywinks and Old Maid were the Words with Friends and Twister of the early twentieth century. Here are the games that Edwardians loved to play.

THE GAME OF PETER CODDLES

The Game of Peter Coddles is a fill-in-the-blank game of words and phrases. The game is based on a book about the New York City adventures of a man from the countryside. The game became popular in the late 1890s as a divide grew between urban and rural residents. City populations were growing, sparked by the Industrial Revolution and an increase in immigrants settling in cities like New York City.

A stack of cards with references written on them—for example, a sea of turtle soup, a pinch of snuff, a daddy longlegs, an old goat, and more—is shuffled and dealt to players, one at a time, until the deck runs out. The phrases are used to complete the narratives in the book.

OLD MAID

In 1904, you could purchase an Old Maid card game for five cents. The game was introduced in the late 1880s. It involves recognizing, matching, and pairing identical cards. Players offer their hand, cards down, to the player on their left, and that player draws a card. As players obtain cards that match other cards in their hand, they set the paired cards aside. The goal is to have the least number of cards at the end, and person left with the Old Maid card is the old maid.

On October 1, 1905, Old Maid was the entertainment for guests during a tea party in Stillwater, Oklahoma. The prize was a teapot. The party was described the next day in the *Daily Democrat* newspaper. Orange ice, cake, ladyfingers, and coffee were served. "Mrs. Fields is an ideal hostess," the story said, "and her social events are always much enjoyed by those who are fortunate enough to be her guests."

BOURSE

Bourse is a stock exchange–inspired card game that was produced by the Flinch Card Company in Kalamazoo, Michigan. Cards were printed with stock-exchange commodities, including beef, corn, wheat, pork, cotton, mutton, and more.

A pack of game cards included eighty cards, ten of each commodity. The game can be played by three to eight players, with one commodity per player. The cards are shuffled and then dealt to the left, one card per player until all of the cards are distributed. Each player arranges their hand according to the commodities that they want to go after in the game. The objective is to acquire a full hand of one commodity. Players trade cards with other players, exchanging the same number of cards, and when one player completes a hand of one commodity, they call out: "Sold!" Ten rounds of the game are played, and the person who has won the most rounds wins the game.

Copies of the game are very rare today; however, it is simple to make. Create your own cards for trading by using graphics of a variety of commodities. Print or cut out card-size trading cards on card stock.

TIDDLYWINKS

Until the 1950s, tiddlywinks had been a game mainly for children. The goal is to get small plastic discs into a bowl by snapping them on their edge. In 1958, the Associated Press announced "tiddlywinks is snowballing" in England. "In Britain, there is a rudimentary literature of tiddlywinks," the story said. The trend was thought to have originated among students at Cambridge University, where there was even talk for a time of advocating for tiddlywinks to become an event in the Olympic Games. In one competition, Oxford beat Cambridge, 113 to 111. Prince Philip of England was asked to join a Cambridge tiddlywinks team, but declined, stating: "While practicing secretly I pulled an important muscle in the second, or tiddly joint, of my winking finger." Polo, he said, would remain his game of choice.

FORFEITS

In the game of forfeits, one player leaves the room. Other players place a piece of jewelry or another personal item in a box in the middle of the room. The player who left the room returns and picks out one item and describes it. To obtain their item back, the owner must contribute a "forfeit," which can be something like singing a song or doing or saying something that is embarrassing to them.

MOVIE TRIVIA

Here is a multiple-choice trivia contest that is based on the 1997 *Titanic* movie directed by James Cameron.

1. WHICH CITY IN WISCONSIN IS JACK DAWSON'S HOMETOWN?

A. Green Bay

B. Wausau

C. Chippewa Falls

D. Onalaska

E. None of the above

2. WHAT DOES ROSE DO WITH THE HEART OF THE OCEAN NECKLACE AT THE END OF THE MOVIE?

A. Give it to her daughter

B. Accidentally step on it

C. Tuck it into her nightgown and go back to bed

D. Drop it into the ocean

E. None of the above

3. WHEN ROSE MEETS JACK FOR DINNER, HOW LONG ARE THE GLOVES THAT SHE IS WEARING?

A. Above the elbow

B. Below the elbow

C. She isn't wearing gloves

D. Wrist-length

E. None of the above

4. DURING DINNER IN FIRST CLASS, HOW DOES JACK DESCRIBE CONDITIONS IN THIRD CLASS?

A. "I haven't been down there yet."

B. "Much better than the squid boat that I worked on in Monterey."

C. "They serve us gruel!"

D. "The best I've seen, ma'am—hardly any rats."

E. None of the above

5. WHEN THE GATES ARE UNLOCKED IN THIRD CLASS, WHAT DOES THE STEWARD SAY?

A. "Women only!"

B. "Follow the green arrows."

C. "One at a time."

D. "Women and children first."

E. None of the above

6. THE KEY THAT CAN OPEN THE HANDCUFFS THAT ARE KEEPING JACK CONFINED IS MADE OF WHAT MATERIAL?

A. Silver

B. Brass

C. Gold

D. Stainless steel

E. None of the above

7. WHEN THE STEWARD WON'T OPEN THE GATE FOR JACK AND ROSE, WHAT DOES JACK DO?

A. He thanks the steward and turns around to go back.

B. He pries a bench away from a wall and uses it to break down the gate.

C. He shakes his fist at the steward.

D. He climbs over the gate.

E. None of the above

ANSWERS

1. C. Chippewa Falls 2. D. Drop it into the ocean 3. A. Above the elbow 4. D. "The best I've seen, ma'am—hardly any rats." 5. A. "Women only!" 6. A. Silver 7. B. He pries a bench away from a wall and uses it to break down the gate.

"We'll both have the lamb, rare,
with very little mint sauce.
You like lamb, right, sweet pea?"

—CAL

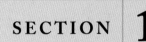

SHOWSTOPPING APPETIZERS

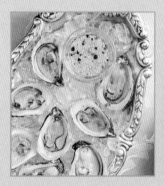

SPRING LAMB WITH MINT SAUCE

When Cal orders for Rose at dinner, Margaret Brown cleverly calls him out about his micromanaging ways. "You gonna cut her meat for her, too, there, Cal?" she asks. The scene is based on the lamb with mint sauce that was among the glamorous entrées on the first-class dinner menu in the hours before the *Titanic* struck the iceberg. The *Titanic* sailed at the beginning of spring, when mint and spring peas would have been among the season's many popular ingredients. The mouthwatering flavors of fresh, vibrant mint and sweet spring peas accent these delicious little lamb lollipops. The carré d'agneau—as the *Titanic's* French culinary staff would have called them—are the rack, or ribs, of the lamb. Arrange the pieces of lamb on a platter with small bowls for the jelly and the pesto. Around the pieces of lamb, tuck in fresh pea shoots and tendrils, fiddlehead ferns, spring violets, or other edible signs of spring.

MAKES 6–8 SERVINGS

MINT JELLY

2 cups fresh mint, chopped

4 cups water

¼ teaspoon fresh lemon juice

4 drops green food coloring

One 1¾-oz box powdered pectin

4 cups sugar

Ingredients continued on following page.

COOK'S TIP: To toast pine nuts, preheat the oven to 350°F. On a lightly buttered pie dish, scatter the pine nuts with a pinch of salt. Place in the oven until fragrant and golden, about 10 minutes. Stir gently after the first 5 minutes.

To make the mint jelly, in a saucepan over high heat, combine the mint with the water. Bring to a boil, then remove the saucepan from the heat and let the mint steep for 15 minutes.

Have ready two 8-ounce glass containers. Using a fine-mesh strainer, strain the mint from the water, reserving the water. Place the mint water back into the saucepan and return it to the stove top over medium heat. Stir in the lemon juice and food coloring. Add the pectin and stir until the powder is dissolved. Stir in the sugar and bring the mixture to a boil. Reduce the heat to low and continue to cook for another 3 minutes. Remove from the heat and pour the jelly into the glass containers. Place the jelly in the refrigerator for 2 hours to set.

While the jellies set, make the pesto. In a food processor or blender, combine all the ingredients and pulse until well-blended. Add oil as needed to reach the desired thickness and consistency. Use right away, or transfer to an airtight container and refrigerate for up to 2 days.

To make the lamb, in a small bowl, mix together the salt, pepper, and half of the garlic. Sprinkle the mixture on top of both sides of each piece of lamb. In a skillet over medium heat, melt the butter, then add the oil. When the oil is hot, place the remaining garlic in the skillet and cook until fragrant, about 1 minute. Add the lamb and cook for 8–10 minutes on each side until a thermometer inserted into the center of the thickest part of the lamb away from the bone registers 125°F.

Recipe continues on following page.

Continued from previous page.

SPRING PEA PESTO

One 12-oz bag frozen peas, thawed

4 tablespoons extra-virgin olive oil

¼ cup pine nuts, lightly toasted

Juice of 1 lemon

2 tablespoons grated Parmesan cheese

½ clove garlic, finely chopped

¼ cup water

½ teaspoon black pepper

½ teaspoon salt

Extra-virgin olive oil, as needed

LAMB

1 teaspoon pink Himalayan sea salt

1 teaspoon freshly ground peppercorns

2 cloves garlic, finely chopped

1 rack of lamb (7–8 cuts of meat from
   each rack; your butcher can cut
   the racks into individual pieces),
   frenched

2 tablespoons butter

2 tablespoons extra-virgin olive oil

Fresh mint sprigs and leaves,
   for garnish

Remove the lamb from the heat and let it rest for at least 5 minutes before serving. (Letting the meat rest will help redistribute the juices for more flavorful, juicier meat.)

Arrange the lamb chops on a platter or decorative tray, then garnish with a scattering of mint sprigs and leaves. Serve with the pesto and jelly.

FRIED CALAMARI WITH PEPPER AND TOMATO SAUCE

This marinara sauce for calamari or other fried seafood is a nod to not only the Italian heritage of Jack's good friend and traveling companion aboard the *Titanic*, Fabrizio de Rossi, but also Jack himself, who worked on a squid boat in Monterey. Scotch bonnet peppers bring five-alarm spice to this sauce, similar to the heat of jalapeño or habanero peppers. Throughout history, Scotch bonnet peppers have been a popular cooking ingredient in Jamaica. Many of the crew members who were working aboard the *Titanic* spent time in Jamaica—sometimes for months—between jobs on ships. First violinist John "Jock" Hume spent several months playing with a band at a resort in Jamaica before working aboard the *Titanic*. He is shown in the scene in which band leader Wallace Hartley is depicted leading the band as they play songs to uplift the passengers as the lifeboats are loaded. "Alright boys, like the captain said, nice and cheery, so there is no panic," Hartley says before leading the band in playing the song "Wedding Dance."

MAKES 8 SERVINGS

SCOTCH BONNET PEPPER MARINARA SAUCE

3 tablespoons extra-virgin olive oil

4 Scotch bonnet peppers, trimmed, seeded, and minced (see Tip)

1 red bell pepper, trimmed, seeded and diced

2 vine-ripened tomatoes, chopped

½ teaspoon sea salt

½ teaspoon black pepper

¼ cup apple cider vinegar

CALAMARI

2 cups all-purpose flour

1 tablespoon hot Hungarian paprika

½ tablespoon ground turmeric

¼ teaspoon coarse sea salt

¼ teaspoon black pepper

1 lb tube calamari, cut into ½-inch rings

4 cups extra-virgin olive oil

To make the marinara sauce, in a skillet over medium heat, heat the oil. Add the peppers and cook, stirring occasionally, until the peppers become tender, about 5 minutes. Add the tomatoes, salt, black pepper, and vinegar. Reduce the heat and simmer until the sauce is thickened, 15–20 minutes. Remove the sauce from the heat and let cool for 30 minutes so that the juices and flavors have time to meld.

While the marinara sauce cools, make the calamari. In a large bowl, stir together the flour, paprika, turmeric, salt, and pepper. Lightly toss the calamari rings in the mixture until completely coated.

Line a serving plate with paper towels and set it next to the stove top. In a skillet over medium-high heat, heat the oil until it registers 325°F on a deep-frying thermometer. Add the calamari rings. Fry until golden brown, 6–8 minutes on each side, then use tongs to transfer the rings to the prepared serving plate and let cool for 5 minutes. Using a paper towel, pat the calamari to absorb some of the oil.

Transfer a pile of the calamari to a serving platter or tray. Place the marinara sauce in a small serving dish and set it on the serving platter with the calamari. Serve right away.

COOK'S TIP: For additional heat, reserve the pepper seeds and add them to taste with the salt and pepper.

JACK

Well, after that, I worked on a squid boat in Monterey. Then I went down to Los Angeles to a pier in Santa Monica and started doing portraits there for ten cents apiece.

ROSE

Why can't I be like you, Jack? Just head out for the horizon whenever I feel like it?

WELSH RAREBIT

First-class passenger Elise Lurette survived the sinking, and in her pocket was the April 12 first-class lunch menu. She had crossed off Welsh Rarebit and Eggs Omar Pacha. Welsh Rarebit can be made with beer or wine. You could make it with Wrexham Lager, which is the pilsner beer that was served aboard the *Titanic*. If you cannot locate Wrexham, a good, dark stout beer will work well in this recipe.

MAKES 8 SERVINGS

16 slices French baguette

1 Honeycrisp apple, thinly sliced

1 beefsteak tomato, thinly sliced

6 cups grated Swiss or Cheddar cheese

4 tablespoons stoneground or
   spicy mustard

1 cup dark stout beer

1 teaspoon dry mustard

1 tablespoon Hungarian paprika ,
   plus 1 pinch for serving

½ teaspoon Worcestershire sauce

1 pinch pink Himalayan sea salt

1 pinch freshly ground peppercorns

Preheat the oven to 350°F.

Using a toaster oven, toast the bread slices. Transfer the toasted bread to a broiler pan and place a slice of apple or tomato on top of each piece.

In a small saucepan over medium heat, combine the cheese, mustard, beer, dry mustard, paprika, Worcestershire sauce, salt, and pepper and stir gently until the cheese melts. When the cheese is completely melted and the mixture is warmed through, remove from the heat. Using a spoon, cover the toasted bread slices with the cheese mixture.

Bake until the cheese bubbles a bit and the edges begin to brown lightly, about 10 minutes. Remove from the oven, sprinkle with the paprika, and transfer to a serving plate. Serve right away.

SOUSED HERRINGS IN LEMON-THYME SAUCE

Yarmouth Bloaters were on the second-class breakfast menu on April 11. Shortly after noon, at 1:30 p.m., the *Titanic* left Ireland from Queenstown—now called Cobh—and set out for New York City. Yarmouth Bloaters are similar to smoked herring. This lemon-thyme sauce is a bright, fresh sauce to add lightly to a plate of smoked herrings. White wine vinegar balances the salty flavors in fresh sardines or anchovies.

MAKES 8 SERVINGS

2 tablespoons butter

1 small shallot, minced

½ red bell pepper, very finely diced

2 tablespoons whole-grain mustard

1 cup Pinot Grigio

Juice of ½ lemon

5 fresh lemon-thyme or thyme sprigs

¼ teaspoon sea salt

¼ teaspoon freshly ground multicolor
   peppercorns

1 lb canned herrings, sardines,
   or anchovies

Variegated radicchio, thinly sliced,
   for garnish

In a medium saucepan over medium heat, melt the butter. Add the shallots and bell pepper and cook for 2 minutes, then add the mustard and wine, stirring to combine. Add the lemon juice and thyme and stir to combine. Add the salt and pepper. Reduce heat to low and let the sauce simmer, stirring occasionally, until it thickens, about 10 minutes.

Arrange the herrings on a platter and drizzle the sauce over the top, or arrange the herring on individual appetizer plates and drizzle the sauce over the top. Garnish with slices of variegated radicchio.

OYSTERS WITH MIGNONETTE SAUCE

The last dinner served in the first-class dining room began with oysters. The menus that survived do not indicate whether a sauce was served with the oysters, but it is a safe bet that a classic French mignonette sauce accompanied them. This mignonette sauce is made with Champagne vinegar, making it a light, bright addition to any type of oysters, whether they are steamed, boiled, or raw.

MAKES 6 SERVINGS

½ cup Champagne vinegar

1 shallot, finely diced

½ teaspoon pink Himalayan sea salt

½ teaspoon freshly ground multicolor peppercorns

½ teaspoon sugar

12 oysters

Combine all the ingredients except for the oysters in a small bowl and whisk until well blended. Place the oysters on a large serving platter covered with crushed ice. Using a spoon, drizzle a little sauce over each oyster and serve immediately.

COOK'S TIP: Oysters are an elegant starter, but they can seem challenging to open at first. To open oysters more easily, you could steam or boil them. First, run each oyster under water to rinse off any sand or grit. To steam the oysters, fill a Dutch oven with about 2 inches of water. Place 6–8 oysters in a steaming basket and place in the Dutch oven over medium heat. Bring the water to a boil and steam the oysters for 6–8 minutes. Transfer the oysters to a plate and let cool on the counter. When they are cool enough to touch, use an oyster shucking knife to open them.

The oyster will be attached to the rounder side of the shell. Place the rounder side of the oyster on a towel. The hinge is on the narrow side of the oyster, at the tip. Wrap the towel around the oyster, with the hinge exposed. Angle the oyster up so that the hinge is raised. Slip the shucking knife into the hinge, and run it along the shell. Run the shucking knife under the oyster to disconnect it from the shell, then pull the top shell up.

FIRST-CLASS LUNCH
CHEESE BOARD

First-class passengers Ruth Dodge and Abraham Salomon both saved first-class lunch menus from April 14. The menu selections included potted shrimps, chicken Maryland, and custard pudding, among other things, and at the bottom of the menu were the words "Iced, draught Munich Lager Beer, 3. & 6 d. a Tankard." The menu also featured an array of eight carefully chosen cheeses. The cheese assortment included soft, hard, and spreadable cheeses, and a variety of flavors, textures, and colors were represented. Except for Cheddar, the cheese assortment did not rotate.

Although it is unclear whether passengers were served accoutrements alongside the cheese selections, a typical modern-day cheese board combines a range of sweet and savory items that pair nicely with the cheeses selected. When in doubt about which cheeses and accoutrements to choose, ask your local cheesemonger for recommendations.

CHEESES SERVED ON THE FIRST-CLASS LUNCH MENU, APRIL 14

Camembert: a ripened soft creamy cow's milk cheese from Normandy, France

Cheddar: a hard, tender cow's milk cheese from Cheddar, England

Cheshire: a hard, crumbly cow's milk Cheddar cheese from Cheshire, England

Edam: a mild semihard cow's or goat's milk cheese from Edam, Holland

Gorgonzola: a soft cow's milk blue cheese from Gorgonzola, Italy

Roquefort: a semihard blue sheep's milk cheese from Southern France

Stilton: a semisoft blue cow's milk cheese from Derbyshire, Ireland

St. Ivel: a spreadable cow's milk cheese from the United Kingdom

SWEET ACCOUTREMENTS

Fresh fruit such as red or green grapes, figs, apples, or berries

Dried fruit such as golden raisins, cranberries, or apricots

Spreads such as honey, apple butter, quince paste, or preserves

SAVORY ACCOUTREMENTS

Cured meats such as chorizo, prosciutto, or salami

Pickled or brined ingredients such as cornichons or olives

Roasted and salted nuts such as almonds, pistachios, or pecans

Sliced baguette, water crackers, or other crackers

Recipe continues on following page.

Continued from previous page.

For a showstopping cheese board fit for royalty (or first-class passengers on a luxury steamship), pick a mixture of 3–5 cheeses ranging from soft to hard. In general, plan on serving 1–2 ounces of each cheese per person. For example, if serving 4 guests, buy 4–8 ounces of each cheese selected. Avoid buying presliced cheeses whenever possible, as they tend to dry out quicker.

Arrange your cheeses on the board and cut small chunks from the block, using separate knives for each cheese to avoid contamination. Fill the board with the desired accoutrements. Cover and refrigerate the board for up to 4 hours. An hour before serving, remove the board from the refrigerator to allow the cheeses to come to room temperature.

 # FIRST-CLASS CAVIAR BAR

When Jack is offered caviar during dinner in first class, he assumes a knowing air that makes him come across with confidence: "No caviar for me, thanks. Never did like it much." Caviar is one of the most luxurious treats in the world. As impressive as caviar is as a party food, it is simple to prepare and serve with toast points, blinis, and an assortment of toppings.

MAKES 8 SERVINGS

6 large eggs, hard-boiled (page 99)

¼ red onion, finely diced

¼ cup finely chopped chives

2 cups crème fraîche or sour cream

½ lb caviar

2 lemons, cut into wedges

1 bunch curly-leaf parsley, stems removed

24 blinis or toast points (without crusts)

Separate the whites from the yolks of the eggs and place in separate small glass serving bowls. Using a fork, mash the whites and the yolks. Place the onion, chives, crème fraiche, and caviar into individual small glass serving bowls.

Fill a wide shallow bowl with crushed ice. Place the bowl of caviar in the middle and place the bowls with the toppings around the caviar. Scatter lemon wedges and parsley around the caviar and toppings.

Line a basket with a cloth and place the blinis and toast points inside.

To assemble, place a dollop of crème fraîche on a blini or toast point. Use an ivory caviar spoon to place a small scoop of caviar on top of the crème fraîche. Sprinkle the desired toppings over the caviar, then squeeze a lemon wedge over the top.

COOK'S TIP: Caviar can also be a topping for Deviled Eggs (page 99).

"Are these all for me?"

—JACK (looking at his silverware for dinner)

"Just start from the outside
and work your way in."

—MOLLY

SECTION  2

SOUPS,
SALADS &
SIDES

SPRINGTIME CONSOMMÉ JARDINIÈRE

The *Titanic* arrived in Cherbourg, France, from Southampton, England, at 6:40 p.m. on April 10. "At Cherbourg," narrates Rose Calvert in the movie, "a woman came aboard named Margaret Brown. We all called her Molly. History would call her 'The Unsinkable Molly Brown.'" In addition to Margaret Brown, John Jacob Astor IV and his bride, Madeleine, boarded at Cherbourg along with more than two hundred other passengers.

Ninety minutes after arriving, the ship left for Queenstown, Ireland, now called Cobh. On that day, first-class passengers ate consommé jardinière. A clear, light broth made from vegetables and chicken, beef, or fish, consommé appeared frequently on Edwardian tables, especially at lunchtime. This recipe celebrates spring with spring peas, spring onions, new potatoes, baby parsnips, and pretty pastel-colored radishes, but any variety of favorite vegetables will work well. A lemon garnish makes the soup bright and light.

MAKES 4 SERVINGS

1 tablespoon butter

2 tablespoons extra-virgin olive oil

½ cup finely diced new potatoes

½ cup finely diced baby parsnips

1 clove garlic, minced

½ teaspoon salt

One 32-oz carton homemade or store-bought vegetable or chicken stock (see Tip)

2 cups water

1 cup spring peas

1 cup finely sliced spring onions

½ cup finely sliced Easter egg radishes or watermelon radishes

Freshly ground peppercorns, for garnish

Fresh lemon-thyme sprigs, for garnish

Lemon slices, for garnish

In a Dutch oven over medium heat, melt the butter. Add the oil, potatoes, and parsnips and cook, stirring occasionally, until the vegetables are slightly soft, about 5 minutes. Add the garlic, salt, stock, and water and bring to a boil. Reduce the heat to low and simmer until the vegetables are tender, about 15 minutes. Add the peas, onions, and radishes and cook until heated through, about 5 minutes longer.

Ladle the soup into bowls. Garnish each bowl with pepper, a sprig of lemon thyme, and a lemon slice and serve.

COOK'S TIP: Traditional consommés call for clarifying the stock before the soup is assembled. Protein—typically two egg whites mixed with ½ lb meat per 1 quart of stock—are combined and brought to a boil, then reduced to a simmer for about 30 minutes. The protein rises to the surface of the stock, absorbing impurities, and forms an omelet-like film. The stock is then strained through a sieve (and the contents of the sieve are discarded), leaving behind a clear, lightly flavored stock. Because it can be a costly and wasteful process, this recipe calls for commercial stock.

TURKEY FRAME SOUP
WITH MINT

Kate Buss was among a group of second-class passengers who organized an impromptu hymn service shortly before the *Titanic* struck the iceberg. The service was led by Reverend Ernest Carter. On April 16, from aboard the rescue ship *Carpathia*, Kate wrote in a letter, "Sunday evening we had a hymn singing congregation; no set service; it was lovely. We met the Dr. P. who was told off by his friend to look out for my ship friend, Miss W[right]., and took him in with us. Another acquaintance, a young fellow, so nice, Mr. [Robert] N[orman] played the piano." There were pianos in both first- and second-class dining saloons for Sunday services. She continued: "Strange to say . . . although we didn't quite realize it, every prayer and hymn seemed to be preparing us for that awful experience."

Shortly before the hymn service that night, roast turkey and cranberry sauce had been served for dinner in second class. After the turkey was roasted, the frame of the turkey was likely saved to create soup stock. A turkey frame will keep in the freezer for several months. The frame of a 15- to 18-pound turkey will produce enough delicious, heartwarming broth to make several batches of soup to have on hand for winter.

MAKES 12 SERVINGS

1 turkey frame, from one 18-pound turkey

8 cups water

4 tablespoons chopped fresh basil

2 bay leaves

3 tablespoons chopped fresh mint, plus 1 tablespoon for garnish

2 tablespoons chopped fresh parsley

1 teaspoon pink Himalayan sea salt

1 teaspoon multicolor peppercorns

1 clove garlic, minced

2 cups chopped turkey meat

2 cups chopped carrots

2 cups chopped celery

1 red bell pepper, seeded and chopped

1 cup chopped red onion

1 cup sliced mushrooms

2 cups chopped fresh or canned tomatoes

2 cups cooked wild rice

In a stockpot over medium-high heat, combine the turkey frame with the water, basil, bay leaves, mint, parsley, salt, and pepper. Bring to a boil, skimming off any foam that forms on the surface, about 30 minutes. Reduce the heat to medium-low and simmer, partially covered, for about 90 minutes.

Remove the frame and set aside. Strain the broth into a large bowl or pot. When frame is cool enough to do so, pull the meat from bones and add it to the 2 cups of chopped turkey meat. Be very careful to make sure that no bones, or slivers of bone, remain in the broth.

Return the broth to the stockpot over medium-high heat. Add the garlic, turkey meat, carrots, celery, bell pepper, onion, mushrooms, and tomatoes. Bring to a boil, then reduce the heat to medium-low and simmer, partially covered, for 30 minutes. Add the cooked rice and cook until heated through. Ladle the soup into bowls and serve.

COOK'S TIP: When you're prepping ingredients, save the trimmings of celery stalks, carrots, onions, and other vegetables and store them in the freezer until you're ready to make broth. In a stockpot over medium heat, combine the vegetables, frame of a chicken or turkey (optional), and a mix of onions, carrots, celery, smashed garlic cloves, and an assortment of fresh herbs such as parsley, sage, rosemary, thyme, oregano, and basil. Add 8 cups of water and bring to a boil over medium-high heat, skimming off any foam that forms on the surface if using chicken or turkey bones. Skim the foam occasionally for the first 30 minutes. Reduce the heat to medium-low and simmer, partially covered, to blend the flavors, 4–6 hours for poultry-vegetable stock, or 1–2 hours for vegetable stock. Strain the stock, taste it, and add salt if needed.

BEET & APPLE SALAD
WITH HONEY DRESSING

On the last day that the *Titanic* sailed, beets were on the first-class lunch menu. The beets were among a buffet of lunch foods that included lettuce, tomatoes, salmon mayonnaise, potted shrimps, anchovies, herrings, sardines, roast and spiced beef, veal and ham pie, Virginia and Cumberland ham, bologna, brawn, and corned ox tongue. This colorful and refreshing recipe is a great addition to a green salad or on its own. As a side salad, serve it on a bed of lettuce greens. The nuts can be made up to two days in advance.

MAKES 4 SERVINGS

CANDIED NUTS

½ cup roughly chopped walnuts or pecans

2 tablespoons extra-virgin olive oil

2 tablespoons firmly packed light brown sugar

1 tablespoon ground turmeric

HONEY DRESSING

6 tablespoons extra-virgin olive oil

2 tablespoons apple cider vinegar

1 teaspoon honey

1 teaspoon sea salt

½ teaspoon black pepper

BEET-APPLE SALAD

6 medium beets, peeled and cut into matchsticks

3 medium apples, peeled and cut into matchsticks

1 bunch green onions, chopped

Preheat the oven to 375°F.

To make the nuts, place them in a baking dish and drizzle the oil over them. Sprinkle the sugar and turmeric over the nuts and stir until thoroughly coated. Bake until the nuts are fragrant and golden, about 8 minutes, then stir the nuts and return to the oven until the nuts are deep golden, about 8 minutes longer. Remove and set aside to cool. Transfer to an airtight container and keep at room temperature until needed.

To make the salad dressing, in a small bowl, combine the oil, vinegar, honey, salt, and pepper. Whisk vigorously until the ingredients are blended thoroughly, about 1 minute.

To make the salad, combine the beets and apple matchsticks in a medium bowl and toss them together lightly. Add the salad dressing and toss until well coated. Transfer to an airtight container and refrigerate for 10–12 hours so the beets have time to marinate. Before serving, sprinkle with the green onions and candied pecans.

> COOK'S TIP: Make a double batch of candied nuts on their own and mix them into a batch of Spicy Caramel Corn (page 93) for a delicious movie snack.

VIOLET CAULIFLOWER TABBOULEH

Tabbouleh is a classic Levantine salad made with parsley, tomatoes, mint, onion, lemon, and olive oil. By some estimates, there were nearly 150 Syrian passengers in third class aboard the *Titanic*. The film nods to their presence when Jack and Rose run past a Syrian woman with two children saying "yalla, yalla," meaning *hurry up*, to a man desperately trying to translate a cabin sign. Traditionally, the salad is made with bulgur; here, finely chopped purple cauliflower is used instead of bulgur, inspired by the cauliflower and pork loin served in first class.

MAKES 6 SERVINGS

1 head purple cauliflower, cut into florets

1 bunch fresh flat-leaf parsley, chopped

1 red onion, chopped

1 clove garlic, chopped

2 tablespoons extra-virgin olive oil

1 tablespoon honey

1 teaspoon fresh orange juice

1 teaspoon fresh lemon juice

Pink Himalayan sea salt and black pepper, to taste

In a food processor, combine the cauliflower, parsley, onion, and garlic and pulse until the mixture becomes like confetti or cauliflower rice, about 10 pulses. Transfer the mixture to a salad bowl.

In a small bowl, combine the oil, honey, orange juice, lemon juice, salt, and pepper. Whisk vigorously until blended thoroughly, about 1 minute. Drizzle the dressing over the cauliflower mixture, toss until lightly coated, and serve.

TRIVIA

With so much excitement surrounding the building and launch of the *Titanic*, many passengers and crew members wrote letters home describing the décor and food on board. Letters were mailed from Queenstown and Cherbourg, the final ports of call before the *Titanic* sailed to New York City. One such letter came from first-class passenger Adolphe Saalfeld. Writing to his wife, Gertrude, he said, "I had quite an appetite for lunch: soup, filet of plaice, a loin chop with cauliflower and fried potatoes; apple Manhattan and Roquefort cheese, washed down with a large spaten beer, iced. So far, see, I am not faring badly."

 # TURNIP PURÉE WITH GINGER

"Where to, Miss?" Jack asks Rose as he honks the horn of a twenty-five-horsepower Renault automobile in the cargo hold of the *Titanic*. "To the stars," Rose breathlessly replies. The Renault was the only automobile aboard the *Titanic*. The man who drove the vehicle, professionally, was second-class passenger Augustus Aldworth, an English chauffeur to the family of William and Lucile Carter of Bryn Mawr, Pennsylvania. On the last night aboard the *Titanic*, puréed turnips were on the second-class dinner menu. More delicate and tender than hearty winter root vegetables such as beets, springtime root vegetables such as turnips, parsnips, and daikon radishes are satisfying yet not overly filling. While it substitutes parsnip for potato, this recipe could work as an adapted neeps and tatties—turnips and potatoes—essential in a Burns Night supper celebrating the Scottish poet.

MAKES 6 SERVINGS

4 cups plus 1 tablespoon milk

4 medium turnips, peeled and chopped into 2-inch pieces

2-inch piece ginger, peeled and diced

1 clove garlic, minced

¼ teaspoon sea salt, plus more for salting the water

½ teaspoon freshly ground multicolor peppercorns, plus more for seasoning

6 cups water

2 medium parsnips, peeled and chopped into 2-inch pieces

2 tablespoons unsalted butter

In a large saucepan over medium-low heat, bring the 4 cups milk to a boil. Add the turnips, ginger, garlic, salt, and pepper. Boil for 3 minutes, then reduce the heat to low and cook until the turnips are soft when poked with a fork or knife, about 7 minutes longer.

Remove the saucepan from the heat and set aside for 30 minutes to let the ginger to steep.

Strain the turnips and place them in a blender with 1 tablespoon of milk. Pulse the blender until the turnips reach the consistency of a purée. Transfer the puréed turnips to a serving bowl.

In a medium saucepan over medium heat, bring the water to a boil. Add a pinch of sea salt. Add the parsnips and boil for 5 minutes. Remove from the heat, then strain the parsnips and set aside to cool slightly. While the parsnips are still warm, add the butter then mash them with a potato masher.

Fold the parsnips into the puréed turnips. Season with pepper and serve.

"I've got everything I need right here with me. I've got air in my lungs and a few blank sheets of paper. I mean, I love waking up in the morning not knowing what's going to happen or who I'm gonna meet, where I'm gonna wind up. Just the other night, I was sleeping under a bridge and now, here I am on the grandest ship in the world having Champagne with you fine people."

—JACK

BOILED HOMINY

"Good voyage up to now!" second-class saloon steward Jacob Gibbons scribbled on a quick postcard to a friend after breakfast on April 11. Well after breakfast, the *Titanic* dropped her anchor at Roches Point in Queenstown (present-day Cobh), Ireland. A dispatch of mail was sent from the *Titanic* to be mailed from Queenstown—including Gibbons's postcard. The menu from the breakfast, printed on the postcard, included boiled hominy among other things. Hominy—dried field corn, boiled or steamed—was a customary Edwardian breakfast food. Soaking hominy in an alkaline liquid results in big, puffy, softened corn kernels that are best eaten cold with other ingredients, such as a citrus vinaigrette dressing, as in this recipe. Hominy is also good in hearty and filling soups, chilies, stews, and casseroles.

MAKES 6 SERVINGS

3 cups cooked rice

Two 15-oz cans white hominy, drained and rinsed

One 28-oz can peeled and diced San Marzano tomatoes

1 bunch green onions, white and green parts finely chopped

1 shallot, diced

6 tablespoons extra-virgin olive oil

2 tablespoons white wine vinegar

1 tablespoon honey

2 oranges

1 pinch sea salt

¼ teaspoon freshly ground peppercorns

In a large serving bowl, mix together the cooked rice, hominy, tomatoes, green onions, and shallot.

In a small bowl, combine the oil, vinegar, honey, juice of 1 orange, salt, and pepper. Whisk vigorously until all ingredients are blended thoroughly, about 1 minute. Toss the dressing with the salad until evenly coated. Cut the other orange into slices, scatter the slices over the salad, and serve.

TRIVIA

On the night the *Titanic* sank, three days after Jacob Gibbons had mailed his postcard, he helped passengers into lifeboat number 11. He manned it until its passengers were picked up by the *Carpathia*. Gibbon's next message home was a telegram that read: "SAFE, STOP. WELL, STOP, DADDY, STOP."

"Why do they always insist on announcing dinner like a damn cavalry charge?"

—MOLLY

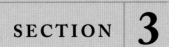

MAIN COURSES

TO REMEMBER

SALMON, MOUSSELINE SAUCE

As he dined with Rose, her family, and Margaret Brown, White Star Line Chairman and Managing Director Bruce Ismay said of the *Titanic*: "She is the largest moving object ever made by the hand of man in all history!" Ismay ordered the salmon. Poached salmon with mousseline sauce was served after the soup course—consommé Olga and cream of barley—during the last dinner in first class aboard the *Titanic*. An Edwardian favorite, mousseline sauce is a classic Hollandaise sauce carefully folded with heavy cream that has been whipped into a thick, pillowy fluff. Mousseline is wonderful over baked fish as well as steamed asparagus, Brussels sprouts, green beans, and other hearty vegetables. In this recipe, fresh tarragon discreetly adds a bright, earthy flavor. While its flavor is pronounced, the herb is not overpowering.

MAKES 4 SERVINGS

SALMON

4 tablespoons butter, plus more for the dish

4 fresh salmon fillets, each 6oz.

Juice of 2 lemons

Salt and black pepper

4 large fresh tarragon sprigs

MOUSSELINE SAUCE

3 large egg yolks

1 cup butter, melted

2 large fresh tarragon sprigs

Juice of 1 lemon

¼ teaspoon sea salt

½ cup freshly whipped cream

COOK'S TIP: When making the mousseline sauce, be careful not to overfold the cream into the sauce so it does not break. Whisking the egg yolks over too much heat could cause them to cook.

To make the salmon, preheat the oven to 375°F. Butter a baking dish large enough to accommodate the fillets.

Place the fish in the dish, skin side down. Drizzle the lemon juice over the fish. Season the fish with salt and pepper, then place 1 tablespoon of the butter and a sprig of tarragon on top of each fillet.

Bake until the fish becomes flaky all the way through, about 40 minutes. Transfer the fish to a serving dish.

Meanwhile, make the sauce. In a saucepan over low heat, whisk the egg yolks and 2 tablespoons of the melted butter. Roughly chop the tarragon to release the flavors and add to the saucepan. Add the remaining butter slowly, 1 teaspoon at a time, stirring continuously, until the sauce becomes thickened, creamy, and glossy, about 5 minutes. Add the lemon juice and salt and continue stirring until thickened and thoroughly combined, about 5 minutes longer. Remove the sauce from the heat.

In a large bowl, using an electric mixer, beat the heavy cream on medium speed until soft peaks form, about 5 minutes. Gently fold the cream into the sauce.

Pour some of the sauce over the fish on the serving dish and serve the remaining sauce in a sauceboat or pitcher on the side.

BAKED HADDOCK, SHARP SAUCE

On the last night aboard the *Titanic*, second-class dinner included baked haddock and sharp sauce. In this recipe, paprika, made from ground dried red peppers, provides flavor that is as pronounced as the flavor of a sharp sauce, yet natural and subtle enough that the flavor is more blended and understated. The lemons balance out the flavors and bring all the ingredients together. As they become acquainted, Jack tells Rose about the fateful day when he fell through the ice while ice fishing as a boy in Chippewa Falls, Wisconsin. There is no way that Jack could have caught haddock while ice fishing in Wisconsin—haddock is a saltwater fish—but this recipe is similar to the deep-fried haddock found on menus in Chippewa Falls and all over Wisconsin, especially on Fridays during Lent.

MAKES 4 SERVINGS

COMPOUND BUTTER

1 cup butter

1 large lemon

1 tablespoon paprika

HADDOCK

4 tablespoons unsalted butter, plus
  more for the dish

4 fillets fresh haddock, each 6–8 oz

Juice of 2 lemons

Sea salt and black pepper

To make the compound butter, place the butter in a bowl and let it sit out on the counter for a few hours to soften. Using a fork, stir in the juice from 1 lemon and the paprika until well blended. Place the butter mixture aside to set and cool to room temperature.

To make the haddock, preheat the oven to 375°F. Butter a baking dish large enough to accommodate the fillets. Place the fish in the dish, skin side down. Drizzle lemon juice over the fish (the juice of about ½ lemon per fish fillet, depending on the size of each fillet). Sprinkle the fish with salt and pepper, on both sides, then place 1 teaspoon of butter on top of each fillet.

Bake until firm and flaky, about 40 minutes. When the fish appears to be baked thoroughly, check it by inserting a knife into the center of one piece to determine if it is flaky all the way through. Transfer the fillets to serving plates, garnish with a pat of compound butter, and serve.

COOK'S TIP: Compound butters are a simple and versatile way to bring a complexity of flavors and textures to everything from fish to meats and more. Explore making different compound butters with herbs, spices, ginger, horseradish and other roots, peppers, and other ingredients.

ROAST TURKEY

Roast turkey and cranberry sauce was on the menu in second class on the last night aboard the *Titanic*. Edwardians were fans of these classic Thanksgiving dishes year-round, and the dish was likely a nod to the strong American presence aboard the ship. Any time of year, a whole roasted turkey, packed with plenty of herbs, creates a remarkable party centerpiece that your guests will remember. Best of all, it is easy to make and is a fulfilling main course.

Do some homework to make your *Titanic* movie-party turkey special. Have fun finding and visiting a local turkey farm. Around the holidays, many local turkey farms have fresh turkeys available. If your turkey is frozen, thaw it in a refrigerator. The US Department of Agriculture recommends thawing a frozen turkey that weighs 12 to 16 pounds in a refrigerator for three to four days.

MAKES 12 SERVINGS

One 12–16 lb whole turkey

4 lemons, quartered

4 red onions, quartered

2 fresh rosemary sprigs

2 fresh sage sprigs

1 bunch fresh parsley

2 fresh thyme sprigs

2 fresh tarragon sprigs

Extra-virgin olive oil,
    for drizzling

½ teaspoon sea salt

1 teaspoon black pepper

½ tablespoon paprika

3 cups dry white wine

Arrange a rack in the lower third of the oven and remove the upper racks. Preheat the oven to 400°F.

Rinse the turkey and remove the neck, gizzards, and any packaging within the cavity. Transfer the turkey to a roasting pan, breast side up.

Arrange the lemons and onions around the turkey, placing them as snugly around the turkey as possible, as well as inside the cavity. Stuff the rosemary, sage, parsley, thyme, and tarragon in the cavity and under the skin. Drizzle some oil evenly into the cavity and all over the outside of the skin. Sprinkle the exterior of the turkey evenly with the salt, pepper, and paprika. Pour the wine into the bottom of the roasting pan.

Roast the turkey for about 20 minutes per pound. (An 8-pound turkey will need to roast for about 2 hours and 45 minutes.) Ovens vary, so the roasting time may be longer or shorter based on your oven. A meat thermometer inserted into the thickest part of the thigh away from the bone should register 165°F.

When the turkey is ready, remove from the oven and let rest for at least 20 minutes before carving.

COOK'S TIP: Place the bones from the turkey in an airtight container and put it in the freezer. Use it when you want to make Turkey Frame Soup with Mint (page 42) or another recipe that calls for stock. Leave plenty of meat on the bones so that it will simmer off the bones and add meat into the soup.

 # BEER-BATTERED FISH

This recipe for pan-fried fish is deeply rooted in the traditions of the state of Wisconsin, where Jack Dawson grew up. Commonly served at supper clubs on Friday nights, this classic meal typically includes a choice of potato, a salad, or coleslaw—made with either vinegar or salad dressing—and buttered rye bread. The light, fresh batter includes another trademark ingredient of the Badger State: beer. Use either a pilsner, which is light and bright, or a stout, which is stronger and more pungent, depending on what you and your guests prefer. For a true Wisconsin experience, whip up a whiskey or Old Fashioned (page 107) to sip before the meal.

MAKES 4 SERVINGS

1½ cups all-purpose flour

1 teaspoon pink Himalayan sea salt

½ teaspoon black pepper

1 tablespoon hot Hungarian paprika

1 large egg, lightly beaten

1½ cups beer

6 tablespoons extra-virgin olive oil, for frying

3 lb cod, perch, haddock, or other whitefish, cut into fillets

1 lemon, cut into wedges

Store-bought tartar sauce or another dipping sauce

In a large glass bowl, combine the flour, salt, pepper, and paprika. Add the egg and beer and mix until thoroughly combined.

Lay a few paper towels on a plate and set it near the stove top. In a frying pan over medium heat, heat the oil. Dip each fillet of fish in the batter, coating both sides evenly.

When oil is hot, add the fillets to the frying pan. Fry the fish until golden, 8–10 minutes on each side. Transfer the fillets to the prepared plate. Blot the top of the fillets with a paper towel and transfer them to individual serving plates. Serve the fish with the lemon wedges, tartar sauce, or another dipping sauce alongside.

COOK'S TIPS: To make a quick coleslaw to accompany the fish, toss a bag of coleslaw mix with 2 cups of a favorite salad dressing.

For a quick sauce for the fish, in a small bowl, whisk together 1 cup of mayonnaise with 1 tablespoon of fresh lemon juice, ½ teaspoon of black pepper, ¼ teaspoon of salt, ¼ teaspoon of paprika, and 1 tablespoon of pickle relish until thoroughly combined.

JACK

Ever been to Wisconsin?

ROSE

What?

JACK

Well, they have some of the coldest winters around. I grew up there near Chippewa Falls. I remember when I was a kid, me and my father, we went ice fishing out on Lake Wissota. Ice fishing is you know where you—

ROSE

I know what ice fishing is!

JACK

Sorry. You just seemed like kind of an indoor girl.

CURRIED CHICKEN

Curried chicken was on the second-class dinner menu on the last night aboard the *Titanic*. While not nearly as opulent as first class, dinners in second class aboard the *Titanic* were still considered better than those served aboard other steamships at the time. British colonization of India had brought curries to high-society Edwardian tables in the early twentieth century, and it was a welcomed comfort-food feast for weary passengers who had a long way to go before reaching New York, where curries and other Indian foods were known at the time by only well-traveled individuals. The menu item was a high point of conversations as passengers recounted their experiences traveling outside their home countries, which was still quite unusual in 1912. This traditional yellow curry is light and mild, yet full of warm and soothing flavors from garlic, ginger, curry powder, onion, and nutmeg. For more heat, add 1 teaspoon of red pepper flakes or a few habanero or Scotch bonnet peppers.

MAKES 4 SERVINGS

4 tablespoons extra-virgin olive oil

2 large boneless, skinless chicken breasts, cut into 1-inch pieces

2 cloves garlic, minced

¼ cup finely chopped red onion

4 tablespoons mild yellow curry powder

1 tablespoon paprika

¼ teaspoon nutmeg

2-inch piece fresh ginger, peeled and diced

2 pinches sea salt

2 pinches black pepper

1 cup plain yogurt

1 red bell pepper, finely chopped

Chopped fresh cilantro, for garnish

In a large skillet over medium-high heat, heat the oil. Add the chicken and cook until browned, about 4 minutes on each side. Transfer to a plate.

Add the garlic and onion to the skillet and cook until they are translucent and fragrant, about 30 seconds. Add the curry powder, paprika, nutmeg, ginger, salt, and pepper. Add the yogurt and stir it in with the sauce. Scrape up any brown bits at the bottom and along the sides of the skillet. Add the chicken and bell pepper and stir to cover them in the mixture. Partially cover, reduce the heat to low, and cook until the chicken is opaque throughout and the bell pepper is tender, about 1 hour. Garnish with cilantro and serve.

COOK'S TIP: For a well-rounded Indian meal, include naan, toasted for a few minutes in the oven. Create a vegetable side dish by stir-frying chopped cauliflower and peas, then add them to a tomato-based tikka masala sauce and simmer until the vegetables are tender, about 10 minutes.

RED WINE–POACHED FIGS
WITH ORANGE BASMATI RICE

These poached figs are perfect for a *Titanic* movie party under the stars on a warm summer night in the backyard. This recipe gives a colorful, flavor-filled face-lift to the stewed figs and rice that were served at teatime in third class on the last night aboard the *Titanic*. A bit of fresh orange zest and juice makes these mouthwatering figs light and bright, while a gentle simmer in Pinot Noir adds a deep, sophisticated profile. Lightly toasted almond slivers add pops of crunch and texture. Serve them in a pretty wineglass on a colorful plate with a charger. Add a sprig of thyme from your garden for a dash of verdant flavor.

MAKES 4 SERVINGS

18–20 small, ripe figs, quartered if large, halved if small

⅔ bottle Pinot Noir

½ cup slivered almonds

1 tablespoon extra-virgin olive oil

½ teaspoon ground cinnamon

½ teaspoon ground nutmeg

½ teaspoon ground cardamom

2 pinches pink Himalayan sea salt

2 pinches black pepper

2 freshly ground cloves

½ tablespoon honey

1 pinch sugar

4 cups cooked basmati rice

1 tablespoon grated orange zest

1 tablespoon fresh orange juice

4 thin strips orange peel, for garnish

Fresh lemon thyme, for garnish

Clean and trim the figs, carefully peeling off the stems.

In a saucepan over medium heat, combine the figs and the Pinot Noir and bring to a boil. Reduce the heat to medium-low and simmer until the figs soften, about 10 minutes.

Preheat the oven to 375°F. In a small pan, toss the almonds with the oil, cinnamon, nutmeg, cardamom, salt, pepper, cloves, honey, and sugar until well coated. Toast the almonds in the oven until the edges are browned, about 10 minutes, stirring the almonds after the first 5 minutes.

Using a strainer, drain the figs from the wine, reserving the liquid, and transfer the figs to a medium bowl. Add the rice and toss gently to combine. Return the wine to the stove and simmer over low heat until reduced by one-third.

To serve, spoon the figs and rice into 4 wineglasses. Sprinkle the toasted almonds, orange zest, and orange juice on top of each. Garnish with a strip of orange peel, a drizzle of the thickened wine mixture, and a few tiny leaves of lemon thyme.

PIZZA WITH RAMPS & SPRING MUSHROOMS

Italian immigrant Fabrizio de Rossi was Jack Dawson's third-class traveling companion aboard the *Titanic*. Around the time that the *Titanic* sailed, New Yorkers were getting their first taste of the foods of Italy, including pizza, as New York's Little Italy began to take hold. In 1897, in New York City, Gennaro Lombardi had just established Lombardi's, the first-known pizzeria in the United States. The pizza trend that Lombardi sparked spread rapidly. The food was especially favored among workers who relied on pizza as a quick lunch option because it was easy to pack and carry. Pizza is still a popular meal, largely because of its versatility, but also because it tastes so good. This pizza celebrates ramps, spring mushrooms, and more of the seasonal ingredients that were ubiquitous aboard the *Titanic*. Have fun exploring with these toppings, or consider other spring ingredients such as morels, green onions, new potatoes, or early peas.

MAKES 2 MEDIUM PIZZAS

One 8-oz package pizza dough

10 tablespoons extra-virgin olive oil
(4 for crust; 6 for tomato sauce)

8–10 vine-ripened or Roma
tomatoes, cut into 1-inch pieces

2 cloves garlic, minced

4 fresh oregano sprigs, leaves
removed from stem

1 teaspoon black pepper

1 teaspoon pink Himalayan sea salt

10 medium balls fresh bocconcini

1 bunch ramps

1 cup sliced mushrooms

1 cup freshly grated Parmesan cheese

Preheat the oven to 400°F. Line 2 baking sheets with parchment paper.

Make the dough according to the package instructions (usually calling for 4 tablespoons of oil). Using your hands, press the dough out on one of the prepared baking sheets. Set aside.

Spread the tomatoes evenly on the other baking sheet and drizzle with the remaining 6 tablespoons of oil. Add the garlic, oregano, pepper, and salt and toss until evenly combined. Roast until the tomatoes are bubbly and begin to look like a sauce, about 30 minutes, stirring halfway through.

Using a spoon, spread the tomato sauce evenly on the dough. Halve the bocconcini balls, and arrange on top of sauce. Slice the bottom one-third of the ramps on the diagonal. Arrange the mushrooms and ramps evenly on the pizza. Sprinkle evenly with the Parmesan cheese. Bake until the pizza is bubbly on top and golden brown around the edges, about 30 minutes. Remove from the oven, cut into slices, and serve right away.

> COOK'S TIP: To make a heart-shaped pizza, divide the dough in half. Roll out two oblong-shaped crusts, making sure they are the same length and thickness throughout. Arrange the crusts at an angle, overlapping at the bottom. Press the inside edges together to make one crust. Place the ingredients on top and bake at 400°F until bubbly on top and golden brown around the edges, about 30 minutes.

"Next it'll be brandies in
the smoking room."
—ROSE [low, to Jack]

"Well, join me for a brandy,
gentleman?"
—GRACIE

"Now they retreat into a cloud of
smoke and congratulate each other on
being masters of the universe."
—ROSE [low]

CLASSIC DESSERTS

BAKED APPLES

Baked apples were on the first-class breakfast menu on the last day aboard the *Titanic*. While baked apples can be a delicious item on a breakfast or brunch menu, there is nothing more elegant than providing each guest with their own personal apple for a sweet ending to a lovely meal.

In this recipe, apples are soaked in Irish whiskey before they are baked. The whiskey gives the apples a heightened layer of flavor that makes them taste similar to fruit that has been soaked in whiskey for a steamed English pudding. The apples are soaked briefly, so that they maintain their form to hold in their cores as much brown sugar, butter, raisins, and nuts as possible.

MAKES 4 SERVINGS

2 tablespoons unsalted butter, plus more for the pan

4 large apples

5 cups Irish whiskey

1 cup firmly packed light brown sugar

¼ cup raisins

¼ cup walnuts, chopped

2 cups cinnamon ice cream, store-bought or homemade (page 80), or whipped cream

4 fresh mint sprigs, for garnish (optional)

Preheat the oven to 350°F. Lightly butter a 9-inch pie dish.

Using an apple corer or a knife, remove the stem and core from each apple, pressing the corer almost all the way to the bottom, but leaving the bottom intact so that the apple can hold the ingredients. Place the apples in a large bowl and pour in just enough whiskey to cover the apples (about 4 cups). Reserve the remaining 1 cup of whiskey. Let the apples soak for 1 hour. Remove the apples from the whiskey, reserving the liquid. Place the apples in the prepared pie dish.

In a large bowl, combine the brown sugar, raisins, and walnuts. Divide this mixture into fourths, one for each apple. Stuff one-fourth of the mixture into the core of an apple. Place ½ tablespoon of butter on top of each apple. Pour ½ cup of the reserved soaking liquid into the bottom of the pie dish.

Bake the apples until tender when pierced with a knife, 45–50 minutes.

Remove the apples and let them rest for 15 minutes. Place each apple on its own dessert plate. Top each apple with a dollop of the ice cream and garnish each with a sprig of mint, if using. Serve a shot of the reserved whiskey with each apple.

PANNEKOEKEN

Titanic crew members were served stewed rhubarb and custard on April 14. Crew member Edward Wheelton saved a menu, which was written by hand, from the crew lunch during the *Titanic's* sea trials on April 3. Rhubarb tart was listed on the menu. In England, stewed rhubarb and cream—sometimes called a "rhubarb fool"—is a treat that is as traditional as scones and clotted cream. In this recipe, stewed rhubarb is the main ingredient in a Dutch baby dessert. A Dutch baby dessert is similar to a sweetened version of a Yorkshire pudding or a popover. A hint of lavender adds flavor.

MAKES 6 SERVINGS

ROASTED RHUBARB

3 cups ½-inch rhubarb pieces

1 tablespoon lavender buds

¼ cup firmly packed light brown sugar

1 tablespoon all-purpose flour

CUSTARD

4 large eggs, lightly beaten

⅔ cup whole milk

⅔ cup all-purpose flour

1 tablespoon granulated sugar

1 teaspoon pure vanilla extract

½ teaspoon salt

4 tablespoons unsalted butter

Confectioners' sugar, for dusting

Lavender buds, for serving

Whipped cream or cinnamon ice cream (page 80), for serving (optional)

To make the roasted rhubarb, preheat the oven to 375°F.

In a 10-inch cast-iron skillet, combine the rhubarb, lavender, brown sugar and flour and stir until the rhubarb is thoroughly coated. Roast in the oven until the rhubarb mixture is soft and spreadable, 15–20 minutes. Set aside.

To make the custard, raise the oven temperature to 425°F.

In a large bowl, using an electric mixer or in the bowl of a stand mixer, beat together the eggs, milk, flour, granulated sugar, vanilla, and salt on high speed. Beat until thoroughly combined, 10–15 seconds.

In a 12-inch cast-iron skillet over medium heat, melt 3 tablespoons of the butter. Let the butter bubble and turn dark brown. Pour the butter into the batter and mix well.

Put the remaining 1 tablespoon of butter in the skillet, then place the skillet in the oven until the butter melts. Remove the pan from the oven, swirl the butter to coat the bottom and sides of the pan, and then pour the batter into the pan. Gently fold in two-thirds of the roasted rhubarb. Place the remaining one-third of rhubarb in the center of the Dutch baby.

Bake for 15 minutes, then reduce the oven temperature to 375°F. Continue to bake until the Dutch baby is puffed and golden and a knife inserted into the center comes out clean, 10–12 minutes longer.

Remove the Dutch baby from the oven and let it cool and settle. This will allow the flavors to meld. Cut the dessert into 4-inch-wide slices and place each slice on a dessert plate. Sprinkle confectioners' sugar and a few lavender buds on top of each slice. Serve the slices topped with a dollop of whipped cream, if desired.

HONEY CRÊPES

Crêpes are fun and easy to make, and they are made with ingredients that most people have on hand regularly. Crêpes are also very versatile. They can showcase a wide array of ingredients, savory or sweet. The delicate, thin pancakes can be served flat or rolled, or with all four sides folded over with sweet or savory ingredients inside and on top. The crêpe cake, which is made with at least one dozen crêpes stacked on top of one another, with a filling layered between each crêpe, is a modern trend.

Because crêpes are so simple, the toppings should be kept simple as well. The crêpes should shine. In this recipe, a light drizzle of honey is the star ingredient. Pick out a few of your favorite types of honey to serve as toppings for these crêpes.

MAKES 12 CRÊPES; 6 SERVINGS

1¼ cups whole milk

1 cup all-purpose flour

3 large eggs

2 tablespoons unsalted butter, melted, plus more for the pan

1 tablespoon plus ¼ cup sugar

¼ teaspoon kosher salt

Extra-virgin olive oil, for greasing

2 cups heavy cream

6 tablespoons honey, plus ½ tablespoon to top each crêpe

4 tablespoons fresh lavender, tarragon, or other French herbs

In a blender, combine the milk, flour, eggs, butter, 1 tablespoon of sugar, and the salt. Using a blender to mix all of the crêpe ingredients together will create a smoother, more consistent batter. Process until very smooth, about 1 minute. Cover the batter and refrigerate for 30 minutes.

Lightly butter an 8-inch crêpe pan over medium-low heat, then pour in 2 tablespoons of the batter. Swirl the pan to cover the bottom with the batter. Cook the crêpe until it is golden, about 1 minute. Carefully turn the crêpe and cook until just beginning to brown on the second side, about 30 seconds. When it is finished cooking, the edges of the crêpe will appear lacey and they will start to lift up a bit all around. Transfer the crêpe to a plate and cover with a piece of parchment paper.

Oil the pan after cooking each crêpe, using a paper towel or a light cloth that is partially drenched in one area with oil. Oiling the pan with a cloth between each crêpe, versus pouring oil in each time, will eliminate splatter.

Repeat with the remaining batter, placing a piece of parchment paper between each crêpe. You should have at least 12 crepes.

> COOK'S TIP: Crêpes are endlessly versatile and can be tailored to your guests' palates. Try chocolate-hazelnut spread with cinnamon, sliced fresh fruit such as strawberries or peaches with sweetened cream cheese or ricotta, or lemon curd or fresh-fruit compotes as alternate toppings.

Use right away or cover and refrigerate for up to 1 day.

In a large bowl, using an electric mixer or in the bowl of a stand mixer, beat the heavy cream on medium-high speed until soft peaks form, 12–15 minutes.

Place 2 crêpes on each dessert plate and arrange the plates on the table in a group. Place the honey, whipped cream, and herbs in separate bowls, then place a small spoon in each bowl. Place these bowls around the dessert plates for guests to choose their crêpe toppings or fillings. Set out one dessert plate with the crêpes arranged as an example of how to assemble the crêpes.

APPLE CUSTARD

With its comforting custard and flavorful apple filling, apple custard pie is one of the charming and nostalgic desserts that helps create an Edwardian setting. This recipe includes a classic French custard similar to the custards that would have been made aboard the *Titanic*.

MAKES 8 SERVINGS

APPLE PIE

2 store-bought frozen pie crusts

6 medium Granny Smith apples, (or another type of sour, tart apple), peeled, seeded, and sliced into 1-inch slices

2 tablespoons fresh lemon juice

¼ teaspoon ground cinnamon

¼ teaspoon ground nutmeg

CUSTARD

2 eggs

1 tablespoon milk

½ cup all-purpose flour

1 ½ cups sugar

Preheat the oven to 425°F.

To make the apple pie, thaw the frozen pie crusts just until they are soft enough to roll out with a rolling pin. If you wait until the pie crusts are room temperature, the dough will be sticky and difficult to roll.

While the pie crust thaws, place the apple slices in a large bowl and toss them in the lemon juice just enough to coat them evenly.

To make the custard, in a large bowl using an electric mixer or in the bowl of a stand mixer fitted with the whisk attachment, combine the eggs, milk, flour, and sugar on low speed until ingredients are mixed well enough that they won't splatter, then increase the speed to high. Beat until ingredients are thoroughly combined and the custard is smooth, about 2–3 minutes. Whisk together until the ingredients are thoroughly combined. Set aside.

Using a rolling pin, roll out the dough so that it is large enough to cover a 10-inch pie dish and still have some extra dough over the edge. Make sure that there is enough dough on both the top and bottom so that the edges can be crimped together.

Place the bottom crust in the pie dish. Using a fork, prick holes all over the bottom crust, to create ventilation. Place the apples on top of the bottom pie crust.

In a small mixing bowl, combine the cinnamon and nutmeg. Use your fingers to toss the ingredients together and combine them well. Sprinkle this mixture over the apples, reserving a few pinches of the mixture to sprinkle on top of the pie crust.

Pour the custard evenly over the apples.

Cover the pie with the top pie crust. Using your fingers, crimp the edges of the top and bottom pie crusts together all the way around the dish. Use a sharp knife to cut a small S-shaped curve in the center of the crust, or use a pie bird, for ventilation.

Bake the pie until the crust is crispy and golden brown and some of the pie filling starts to bubble up around the edges, about 50–55 minutes. Store in the refrigerator in an airtight container for 2–3 days.

MOLLY

Hey, uh, who thought of the name *Titanic?*
Was it you, Bruce?

ISMAY

Yes, actually. I wanted to convey sheer size, and size
means stability, luxury, and above all, strength.

ROSE

Do you know of Dr. Freud, Mr. Ismay? His ideas
about the male preoccupation with size might be of
particular interest to you.

ETON MESS

Meringues with freshly whipped cream and fruit sauces were popular Edwardian desserts. The beloved dessert known as Eton mess has been served at boarding school cricket matches since the late nineteenth century. This luscious, creamy dessert is refreshing on a hot summer day and shows off the finest fruits of the season. This recipe is for Eton mess with blueberries. If you pick your own blueberries, include a few blueberry leaves for an unexpected pop of green garnish.

MAKES 6 SERVINGS

MERINGUE

4 large egg whites

1 cup sugar

¼ teaspoon cream of tartar

BLUEBERRY SAUCE

1 cup fresh blueberries

½ cup water

½ cup sugar

1 pinch pink Himalayan sea salt

2 teaspoons cornstarch

Juice of 1 lemon

1 teaspoon grated lemon zest

CREAM

2 cups heavy cream

½ cup sugar

½ teaspoon fresh lemon juice

Preheat the oven to 250°F.

To make the meringue, in a large bowl if using a handheld mixer or in the bowl of a stand mixer, beat the egg whites, sugar, and cream of tartar on low for 5 minutes, then increase the speed to medium and beat until the meringue thickens and soft peaks form, about 5 minutes longer.

Line 2 baking sheets with parchment paper. Divide the meringue in half and spread one half on each sheet in a circle about the size of a round cake pan. Place both baking sheets in the oven until the meringue becomes firm and lightly browned on top, 45–50 minutes.

Meanwhile, make the blueberry sauce. In a medium saucepan over medium heat, combine the blueberries, water, sugar, and salt and bring to a boil, whisking continuously. Reduce the heat to low and simmer, stirring constantly, until the mixture thickens to the consistency of fruit jam, 4–5 minutes. Stir in the cornstarch and lemon juice and cook for I minute more. Stir in the lemon zest, remove from the heat, and let cool. The mixture will become thicker as it cools.

To make the cream, in a large bowl using an electric mixer or in the bowl of a stand mixer, beat together the heavy cream, sugar, and lemon juice on high until thickened, about 3 minutes.

To assemble the dessert, place one of the meringue rounds on a cake plate. Spread half of the blueberry sauce on top. Spread half of the cream on top of the blueberry sauce. Place the other meringue round on top of the layer of cream, spread with the remaining half of the cream, then spread with the remaining half of the blueberry sauce.

PEACH MELBA WITH RASPBERRY SAUCE & CINNAMON ICE CREAM

First-class *Titanic* menu items were largely based on the style of French cuisine that was defined by Auguste Escoffier in the late 1800s and early 1900s. While working in London, Escoffier made his mark with his fresh adaptations and simplifications of Victorian recipes. In the early 1890s, Escoffier created the simple, lovely dessert called peach Melba at the Savoy Hotel in London. Peach Melba was his homage to Australian opera singer Nellie Melba. She was staying at the Savoy while she was in London playing Elsa in the Wagner opera *Lohengrin*. Soon after Escoffier introduced the dessert, it became as much a part of Edwardian pop culture as the woman who inspired it.

MAKES 4 SERVINGS

3 large ripe peaches

2 cups water

1 cup granulated sugar

½ teaspoon pure vanilla extract

RASPBERRY SAUCE

2 cups fresh raspberries

½ cup water

1 tablespoon confectioners' sugar

Juice of ½ lemon

CINNAMON ICE CREAM

2 cups heavy cream

14 oz sweetened condensed milk

¼ cup ground cinnamon

¼ cup granulated sugar

Slice the peaches in half and remove the pits. Fill a large bowl with water and ice.

In a Dutch oven over high heat, bring the 2 cups water to a boil. Using tongs, place the peaches, skin side down, in a single layer in the water. Boil the peaches until the skins begin to loosen, about 2–3 minutes. Using a slotted spoon, transfer the peaches to the ice water to stop the cooking, reserving the water in the pan. Leave the skins on the peaches.

Add the granulated sugar and vanilla to the water in the pan and bring back to a boil over medium-high heat, stirring to dissolve the sugar. Add the peach halves, reduce the heat to low, and simmer, turning the peaches once, until tender when pierced with a knife, 3–4 minutes on each side. Remove from the heat, cover the pan, then let the peaches steep for at least 30 minutes before serving. The peaches can be stored in the syrup in the refrigerator for 3–4 days.

To make the sauce, in a medium saucepan over medium-high heat, combine the raspberries, water, confectioners' sugar, and lemon juice. Bring the mixture to a rolling boil, then reduce to low and simmer, stirring occasionally, until the mixture thickens, 8–10 minutes. Remove from the heat. The sauce will continue to thicken as it cools.

Remove the seeds from the sauce by pouring it through a fine-mesh strainer into a bowl. The sauce can be refrigerated for 3–4 days.

Recipe continues on following page.

Continued from previous page.

To make the ice cream, in a large bowl, using an electric mixer, or in the bowl of a stand mixer, beat the heavy cream on low until the cream becomes thick enough that it will remain in the bowl, about 5 minutes. Increase the speed to medium-high and beat until soft peaks form, 10–12 minutes longer. Gently fold the sweetened condensed milk into the whipped cream. Pour into a 9-by-12-inch shallow cake pan or large loaf pan. Mix the cinnamon and sugar together and gently fold into the mixture to swirl. Cover the cream mixture with waxed paper or parchment paper and place it in the freezer overnight.

To serve, place 2 peach halves in each of 4 individual glass serving dishes. Top each serving with a scoop of the ice cream. Drizzle raspberry sauce on top and serve immediately.

COOK'S TIP: Pour 1 fl oz of fruit schnapps over the scoop of ice cream and top with a maraschino or brandied cherry.

# CHERRY CLAFOUTIS

Clafoutis (pronounced *kla-foo-TEE*) is a crustless baked custard studded with stone fruits. Clafoutis was introduced in the 1800s in France's Limousin region, known around the world for Limoges porcelain, and for the oak barrels produced there for making Cognac. Celebrate the origins of this traditional French dessert by placing a sprig of fresh lavender on each piece. Sprinkling a little bit of confectioners' sugar on top brings the dessert together, but a dollop of whipped cream or ice cream is also delicious as an accompaniment. Create a tradition of serving clafoutis in the summer, when plums, apricots, cherries, and other stone fruits are in season.

MAKES 8 SERVINGS

Butter, for the pan

1 lb fresh dark sweet cherries, pitted and sliced

1 cup whole milk

¼ cup heavy cream

½ cup cake flour, sifted

4 large eggs, at room temperature

½ cup granulated sugar

⅛ teaspoon salt

½ teaspoon almond extract

Confectioners' sugar, for dusting

Ice cream or whipped cream, for serving

Preheat the oven to 350°F. Grease a 9-inch pie dish with butter and arrange the cherries in the pie dish.

In a medium saucepan over medium-low heat, warm the milk and cream. When bubbles begin to form around the sides, remove from the heat and vigorously whisk in the flour, a little at a time, until no lumps remain.

In a large bowl, whisk together the eggs, granulated sugar, and salt. Slowly whisk in the milk mixture and almond extract to make a batter. Pour the batter over the cherries.

Place the dish on a baking sheet and bake until puffed and lightly browned and the edges are pulling slightly away from the dish, 45–55 minutes.

Remove the dessert from the oven and allow it to cool and settle for 15 minutes. Sprinkle some confectioners' sugar on top. Cut into 4-inch-wide pie-shaped slices and serve warm with a scoop of ice cream alongside.

> COOK'S TIP: For a more rustic touch, bake the clafoutis in a 9-inch cast-iron skillet.

PLUM PUDDING

This recipe for steamed English pudding with whiskey-stout plum sauce is a lighter version of the traditional rich, dark plum pudding that was served for supper in third class on the last night that the *Titanic* sailed. Sweet canned cherries, chunks of fresh Honeycrisp apples, and grated orange and lemon zest brighten up this historical dessert.

MAKES 16–18 SERVINGS

PLUM PUDDING

¼ cup golden raisins

¼ cup diced skin-on Honeycrisp apples

¼ cup dried figs

¼ cup chopped dried prunes

¼ cup chopped dried Medjool dates

¼ cup chopped maraschino cherries

¼ cup grated orange zest

¼ cup grated lemon zest

¼ cup grated carrots

½ cup Irish whiskey

½ cup stout beer

½ cup butter, plus more for the pan

1 cup firmly packed light brown sugar

3 large eggs

1 cup bread crumbs

1 cup all-purpose flour

½ teaspoon baking powder

½ teaspoon ground nutmeg

½ teaspoon ground cinnamon

To make the pudding, in a large bowl, combine the raisins, apples, figs, prunes, dates, cherries, orange zest, lemon zest, carrots, whiskey, and beer. Stir to combine well. Cover the mixture and let sit for at least 1 hour, stirring after 30 minutes.

In another large bowl, using an electric mixer on low speed, cream the butter and the sugar until just combined, about 1 minute. Add the eggs, beating on high until combined well, about 1 minute. Add the bread crumbs, flour, baking powder, nutmeg, cinnamon, ginger, salt, and walnuts.

Using a fine-mesh strainer, strain the fruit and carrots and reserve the whiskey-beer mixture. Transfer it to a container and refrigerate until needed to make the whiskey-stout plum sauce.

Add the fruit mixture to the pudding batter. Use one hand to mix the ingredients together. Scrape the sides of the bowl to incorporate all of the ingredients well.

Fill a Dutch oven two-thirds full with water. Bring the water to a boil over high heat, then reduce the heat to medium-high and let the water simmer.

Generously butter a bread loaf pan with handles. Pour the pudding batter into the bread loaf pan. Cover the pan securely with aluminum foil. Be sure to seal the edges tightly all around.

Place the bread loaf pan on top of the Dutch oven vertically, with the handles extending over the edge on both sides. Let the pudding steam over the simmering water until the pudding is firm on top and resembles the consistency of a cake, about 2 hours. Check the water level in the stockpot occasionally and top off with more water as needed.

½ teaspoon ground ginger

¼ teaspoon salt

¼ cup roughly chopped walnuts

WHISKEY-STOUT PLUM SAUCE

8 oz plum jam or jelly

1 tablespoon butter

WHIPPED CREAM

2 cups heavy cream

4 tablespoons sugar

To check if the pudding is cooked, insert a knife into the center. If it comes out clean, the pudding is ready. The edges of the pudding will start to come away from the mold when it is done.

While the pudding cooks, make the sauce. In a saucepan over medium heat, bring plum jam, butter, and reserved whiskey-beer mixture to a boil. Boil the mixture for 3 minutes, stirring continuously. Remove from the heat and let the sauce sit for at least 30 minutes.

While the sauce sets, make the whipped cream. In a large bowl using an electric mixer or in the bowl of a stand mixer, beat together the cream and sugar on low speed for 5 minutes until the cream thickens enough so that it will remain in the bowl, then increase the speed to medium-high and beat until the cream thickens to a whipped cream consistency and forms light peaks, 5–8 minutes longer.

To serve, remove the pudding from the Bundt pan and transfer to a serving platter. Top with whiskey-stout plum sauce and whipped cream.

"Are you ready to go back
to *Titanic*?"

—BROCK LOVETT

SECTION **5**

MOVIE
SNACKS

CARDAMOM MALTED MILK BALLS

On April 17 at a meeting in Lancaster, Pennsylvania, Milton Hershey recalled a whopper of a story about how he narrowly escaped travel on the *Titanic*. The candy-company founder and his wife, Catherine, suddenly needed to return to Pennsylvania and had planned to travel home aboard the *Titanic* from Nice, France. Milton Hershey had even written a check to the White Star Line for $300—10 percent of the cost of a first-class stateroom aboard the *Titanic*. In the end, they opted for a more expeditious route home on the German ship SS *Amerika*. The day before the *Titanic* struck the iceberg, the SS *Amerika* had sent a message to Captain Smith warning of huge icebergs in the area where the *Titanic* sank. Hershey's cancelled check is now in the Hershey Community Archives.

Malted milk is made from malted barley, wheat flour, and evaporated whole-milk powder. In the early 1900s, malted milk powder—introduced by two brothers from England, William and James Horlick, as a nutritional additive—was becoming a trendy flavoring for food. Malts were created at Walgreens in 1922. In 1939, the Overland Candy Company introduced malted milk balls called Giants. Leaf Brands reintroduced them as Whoppers in 1949. In 1996, Whoppers became part of Hershey's. While these treats are reminiscent of the famous candy, a pinch of cardamom gives these homemade movie-theater snacks a twist of spice.

MAKES 12 SERVINGS

One 10-oz bag white chocolate chips or wafers

1 cup malted milk powder, sifted

½ teaspoon ground cardamom, plus more for garnish

One 10-oz bag milk chocolate chips

Place the white chocolate chips in a medium microwave-safe bowl and microwave at medium power, stopping to stir every 20 seconds, just until the chocolate is melted and smooth. Do not overheat the chocolate or it will seize (become thick and lumpy). Remove the chocolate from the microwave and stir.

Add the malted milk powder to the white chocolate and slowly stir them together. Add the cardamom and stir until combined. Cover and refrigerate, stirring occasionally, until cool enough to be scooped out, about 20 minutes.

Using a tablespoon to ensure that the size of each piece is consistent, scoop 1 tablespoon of the white chocolate into your palm. Using your hands, roll the chocolate into a 1-inch ball. Repeat with the remaining chocolate.

Place the milk chocolate chips in another medium microwave-safe bowl and microwave at medium power, stopping to stir every 20 seconds, just until the chocolate is melted and smooth. Remove the chocolate from the microwave and stir.

Place 2 of the milk balls in the melted milk chocolate. Using a large spoon, roll the balls in the milk chocolate, ensuring that they are completely and evenly coated. Place the balls on parchment paper and let them set at room temperature. Repeat with the remaining milk balls. Sprinkle a pinch of cardamom on top of each ball, then serve.

RASPBERRY GUMDROPS

Gumdrops—or spice drops—were already beloved long before the *Titanic*. Orange jelly wedges—gumdrops made with orange flavoring—were an especially popular Edwardian candy. Today, a visit to the movie theater just isn't complete without a handful of the little gummy candies. Make heart-shaped gumdrops for a special snack for a *Titanic* movie screening—possibly on February 15, which is National Gumdrop Day. Though this recipe calls for raspberry flavoring, any of your favorite fruit flavorings will work well here. To make spice drops, replace the 1 tablespoon of raspberry extract with 1 tablespoon of mint, anise, or allspice extract.

MAKES ABOUT 10 LARGE HEART-SHAPED GUMDROPS OR ABOUT 30 SMALL DROPS

Three 1-oz packages unflavored gelatin powder

1½ cups granulated sugar

1 tablespoon raspberry flavoring or extract

1 tablespoon red food coloring

Butter, for the pan

1 tablespoon sugar crystals

1 tablespoon red sanding sugar

In a large bowl, combine the gelatin with ½ cup of cold water and let sit for 10 minutes.

In a small saucepan over medium heat, combine the sugar with 1¼ cups of water and bring to a boil, stirring continuously. Add the gelatin mixture and reduce the heat to low. Simmer, stirring occasionally, until the mixture dissolves completely, about 10 minutes. Remove the mixture from the heat, add the flavoring and food coloring, and stir until thoroughly combined.

Generously butter an 8-inch square cake pan. Pour the gelatin mixture into the pan. Cover and refrigerate until set, at least 4–6 hours or up to 3 days in advance.

Use small heart-shaped cookie cutters to cut out gumdrops, or cut them into little squares using a knife.

In a medium bowl, mix together the sugar crystals and the sanding sugar. Using a spoon, place each gumdrop in the bowl and lightly toss until evenly coated. Transfer to a serving plate and serve.

SPICY CARAMEL CORN

No *Titanic* movie night would be complete without popcorn. Cracker Jack, introduced at the World's Columbian Exposition in 1893 in Chicago, inspired many Americans to make caramel corn at home. One such person was Dan Coxon ("Popcorn Dan"), a third-class passenger aboard the *Titanic* who peddled popcorn and peanuts from a red and yellow Cretor wagon on Main Street in Merrill, Wisconsin—located about 100 miles from Chippewa Falls, Jack's hometown. While in London, he was looking into uniforms for movie theater ushers. He wanted to open the first movie theater in northern Wisconsin. At the *Titanic* resting place, deep on the floor of the Atlantic Ocean, a leather wallet was found intact. The wallet contained coins and bills, one of which was marked "Merrill." In 1912, some local banks produced currency. Dan Coxon did not survive the ship's sinking, and his body was never recovered.

MAKES 16 SERVINGS

1 cup unsalted butter, cut into small pieces, plus more for the pan

1½ cups firmly packed light brown sugar

½ cup light corn syrup

1 teaspoon sea salt

½ teaspoon baking soda

¼ teaspoon ground cayenne

2½ teaspoons pure vanilla extract

16 cups popped popcorn

Preheat the oven to 250°F. Generously butter 2 large baking sheets.

In a heavy saucepan over medium heat, combine the sugar, corn syrup, butter, and salt. Bring to a boil, stirring constantly. Continue to boil for 5 minutes, stirring frequently. Remove the mixture from the heat.

In a small bowl, combine the baking soda and cayenne. Whisk the mixture quickly into the caramel, then add the vanilla. Stir until thoroughly combined. Place the popcorn in a large bowl, then pour the caramel over the popcorn. Gently fold the mixture with the popcorn until the popcorn is evenly coated. Pour the popcorn mixture into the prepared pans.

Bake until the caramel appears baked well into the popcorn, about 30 minutes. Using a spoon, stir the caramel corn every 10 minutes. Remove the popcorn from the oven and let cool to room temperature. Transfer to a serving bowl and serve.

> ENTERTAINING TIP: Fill classic red-and-white striped popcorn boxes with yellow-and-white silk flowers or freshly cut carnations to look like popcorn. Fill others with popcorn: some with caramel, some with butter, and some plain.

JACKET POTATOES

On the last day aboard the *Titanic*, baked jacket potatoes were on the first-class lunch menu. Earlier that day, jacket potatoes had been served for breakfast in third class. Third-class passenger Sarah Roth had tucked away in her purse what might be the only surviving third-class *Titanic* menu. Roth was able to obtain a seat in collapsible lifeboat C, which was rescued by the *Carpathia*, along with William Carter, Bruce Ismay, and four Chinese third-class passengers. On the back of her menu, with a pencil, Roth wrote the numbers of lost and saved passengers.

MAKES 6–8 SERVINGS

15–20 new potatoes, washed

2 tablespoons extra-virgin olive oil

¼ teaspoon sea salt

½ teaspoon black pepper

3 tablespoons roughly chopped fresh
   rosemary

2 cups sour cream

2 cups grated sharp Cheddar cheese

½ cup sun-dried tomatoes

¼ cup sliced sweet pimentos

1 bunch green onions, white and
   green parts sliced

1 shallot, minced

Preheat the oven to 375°F. Line 2 baking sheets with parchment paper.

Position each potato horizontally and slice just enough off the bottom so that the potato stands on a baking sheet. Slice just enough off of the top so that the skin is removed. Place the potatoes in a large bowl.

Toss the potatoes with the oil, salt, and pepper until the potatoes are evenly coated. Place the potatoes slice-side down on the prepared baking sheets and sprinkle the rosemary on top of the potatoes.

Bake the potatoes until tender when pierced with a knife, 25–30 minutes. Transfer to a serving platter. Place the sour cream, cheese, tomatoes, pimentos, green onions, and shallot into individual glass serving bowls. Serve the potatoes with the accompaniments alongside.

ENTERTAINING TIP: Involve guests by asking each of them to bring a favorite baked potato topping. Coordinate a list of the items each guest plans to bring to ensure variety.

BROWNIES

Much of the Edwardian style was inspired by the World's Columbian Exposition, a world's fair held in Chicago in 1893. For the exposition, Bertha Palmer asked the bakers at Chicago's illustrious Palmer House Hotel—owned by her husband—to create a new chocolate treat. Palmer asked that the snack be something that could be easily packed for exposition participants who were on the go throughout the festival. The bakers came up with a cross between a cake and a fudge, and they called it a "brownie." Brownies became the talk of the town all over Chicago and across the United States. Today, brownies are still as popular as they were when they were first created in the Windy City.

These brownies are based on the Palmer House Hotel brownies, but they are made with almonds instead of walnuts, and with sour cream instead of apricot preserves, which makes them a moister, lighter treat. Serve them alone as a movie snack or alongside cinnamon ice cream (page 80) for a decadent finish to an Edwardian-themed dinner party.

MAKES 8 SERVINGS

½ cup unsalted butter, plus more for the pan

4 oz milk chocolate chips

2 large eggs

1 cup sugar

1½ teaspoons pure vanilla extract

Pinch sea salt

⅔ cup all-purpose flour

½ cup sour cream

1 cup slivered almonds

1 cup mini milk chocolate chips

Preheat the oven to 350°F. Butter an 8-inch square cake pan.

In a large microwave-safe bowl, combine the chocolate chips and butter and microwave at medium power, stopping to stir every 20 seconds, just until melted and smooth. Do not over-heat the chocolate or it will seize (become thick and lumpy). Remove the chocolate and stir. Set aside.

In a large bowl using an electric mixer, beat together the eggs and sugar on medium-high speed until thoroughly combined. When the chocolate mixture is at room temperature, add it to the bowl with the eggs and sugar, then add the vanilla, and beat until just blended. Add the salt, flour, and sour cream and beat until thoroughly combined. Stir ¾ cup of the almonds into the batter. Pour the batter into the prepared cake pan. Sprinkle the remaining ¼ cup of almonds and the mini chocolate chips over the top of the batter.

Bake until a toothpick inserted in the center comes out clean, 35–40 minutes. Transfer to a wire rack and let cool completely. Cut into 8 squares and serve.

ASPARAGUS-MUSTARD GOUGÈRES

Gougères (pronounced *goo-jer*) are tiny cheese pastries made with choux dough. Like the eggy quiche Lorraine and the meaty pâté en croûte, these bites are among the examples of the warm, savory pastries distinct to French cuisine. Gougères l'Italianne and au fromage (with cheese) were featured in a menu published in an English newspaper in 1894. The story also listed rhubarb cream, quenelles, consommés, glacées, and other Escoffier-style menu items that were served aboard the *Titanic*. First-class passengers were likely familiar with gougères, because during the Edwardian era, upper-class British cuisine was heavily influenced by French cuisine.

These versatile bites allow for great creativity with ingredients. This recipe showcases asparagus, which was one of the springtime ingredients used aboard the *Titanic*. Asparagus is wonderful on its own or with a light sauce—it was served cold with a vinaigrette for dinner in first class on the night that the *Titanic* struck the iceberg—but asparagus gougères is a mouthwatering adaptation. Robust whole-grain mustard rounds out the flavor profile of these very flavorful—and seasonal—gougères.

MAKES ABOUT 48 PUFFS

2 cups whole milk

8 tablespoons butter, cut into ½-inch pieces

2 teaspoons sea salt

2 cups all-purpose flour

8 large eggs

½ lb Gruyère cheese, shredded

½ cup finely chopped fresh asparagus tips

2 tablespoons whole-grain mustard

COOK'S TIP: To make plain gougères, simply omit the asparagus and mustard and bake as directed.

Preheat the oven to 375°F. Line 2 baking sheets with parchment paper.

In a large heavy saucepan over high heat, combine 2 cups of the milk, the butter, and salt and bring to a boil. Add the flour, reduce the heat to low, and stir with a wooden spoon until the mixture forms a ball and pulls cleanly away from the sides of the pan, about 5 minutes. Remove from the heat and let cool for 2 minutes.

Using an electric mixer on medium speed, add the eggs to the milk-and-flour mixture, one at a time, beating well after each addition until thoroughly incorporated and the dough is smooth and shiny, about 5 minutes. Stir in three-fourths of the cheese, distributing it evenly. Stir in the asparagus and mustard.

Transfer the dough to a pastry bag fitted with a large round tip. Alternatively, you can use a large plastic storage bag with ½-inch of a bottom corner cut off. Roll the sides of the bag down so that you can fill it at the open end. Fill the bag with the pastry, roll the sides back up, and press the dough into the open corner.

Pipe mounds of dough about 2 inches in diameter onto the prepared baking sheets, spacing them about 2 inches apart. You should have about 48 puffs. Sprinkle the remaining one-fourth of the cheese on the pastry mounds.

Bake the pastries until well puffed and golden brown, 30–35 minutes. Serve right away.

DEVILED EGGS

Some of the earliest known references to deviled eggs go back all the way to ancient Rome. The deviled eggs we know best today—the kind made with mayonnaise—first appeared in *The Boston Cooking School Cook Book* by Fannie Farmer in 1896. Within fifteen years, deviled eggs were standard picnic fare. However, it wasn't until the 1940s that mayonnaise became widely used in recipes. For a colorful, flavor-filled plate of deviled eggs, make a basic filling with mustard and mayonnaise. Add hot sauce to some and avocado to others. A soft, spreadable cheese made with herbs or garlic mixed in with a mayonnaise-and-mustard filling is another option for creating deviled eggs with different flavors, textures, and colors.

MAKES 8–12 SERVINGS

1 head oak leaf lettuce,
    leaves separated

24 large eggs

2 cups mayonnaise

½ cup mustard

¼ teaspoon sea salt, plus more
    for seasoning

½ teaspoon black pepper,
    plus more for seasoning

½ teaspoon hot sauce

1 avocado, mashed

6 thin slices hard salami

1 tablespoon minced fresh chives

2 tablespoons chopped fresh parsley

1 teaspoon paprika

Line a large platter with the lettuce leaves.

In a large heavy saucepan over high heat, combine the eggs with water to cover by 1–2 inches and bring to a boil. Remove from the heat, cover, and let stand for 15 minutes. Transfer the eggs to a bowl of ice water and let stand for 15 minutes to stop the cooking.

Peel the eggs. Halve each egg lengthwise. Remove the yolk from each egg, being careful not to break the whites, placing the yolks in a large bowl and transferring the whites to the prepared platter.

Using a fork, mash the yolks. Add the mayonnaise, mustard, salt, and pepper and mix until thoroughly combined. Divide the mixture evenly into 3 bowls. In one bowl, add the hot sauce and mix until thoroughly combined. In another bowl, add the avocado and mix until thoroughly combined. For traditional deviled eggs, do not add ingredients to the remaining one-third of the yolk mixture.

Transfer one of the egg yolk fillings to a pastry bag fitted with a large round tip. Alternatively, you can use a large plastic storage bag, with ½-inch of a bottom corner cut off. Roll the sides of the bag down so that you can fill it at the open end. Fill the bag with the mixture, roll the sides back up, and press the mixture into the open corner. Pipe the filling into the wells of 8 egg whites. Repeat with the second egg yolk filling, using a clean pastry bag.

Place a wedge of salami on top of each of the eggs filled with the hot sauce mixture. Sprinkle all of the eggs evenly with the chives, parsley, and paprika. Season to taste with salt and pepper, then serve.

TEA SANDWICHES

In 1840, Lady Anna Maria Stanhope, seventh Duchess of Bedford, introduced the idea of a late-afternoon pot of tea with some bite-size sandwiches and sweets. The light meal was intended to help hold her over until dinner. Stanhope was a lady-in-waiting to Queen Victoria, and by the late 1840s, the royal household was hosting afternoon teas on a regular basis. The trend caught on quickly and has been popular everywhere ever since. Today, *Titanic*-themed afternoon tea parties—with teas, sandwiches, and sweet treats—are hosted around the world to celebrate this custom. Make these tea sandwiches for an Edwardian-themed movie party, and include some sugary movie snacks such as Raspberry Gumdrops (page 90).

MAKES 16 TEA SANDWICHES

CUCUMBER WITH ORANGE-FENNEL CRÈME FRAÎCHE

2 cups crème fraîche

½ fennel bulb, thinly sliced, fronds finely chopped

1 tablespoon fresh orange juice

¼ teaspoon sea salt, plus more for sprinkling over the cucumber pieces

½ teaspoon black pepper, plus more as needed

¾ English cucumber, thinly sliced and slices quartered

4 thin slices dark rye bread

4 thin slices orange, including peel, for garnish

Ingredients continue on following page.

To make the cucumber sandwiches, in a medium bowl, combine the crème fraîche, fennel, orange juice, salt, and pepper. Allow the mixture to sit for at least 1 hour so that the flavors have time to meld.

In a separate small bowl, sprinkle the cucumber pieces with salt and let stand for 20 minutes.

Lay the bread slices on a work surface. Using a serrated knife, cut off the crusts from each slice. Cut each slice into four 2-inch squares, or use a heart-shaped cookie cutter to make heart shapes. Spread each slice with the crème fraîche mixture, dividing it evenly. Place 2 cucumber quarters on top of each slice.

Arrange the open-faced sandwiches on a serving platter, then garnish each with an orange slice and a sprinkle of the chopped fennel fronds. Sprinkle with black pepper and serve.

To make the cheese sandwiches, in a large bowl, combine the cream cheese, Cheddar cheese, mayonnaise, pimentos, salt, and pepper. Allow the mixture sit for at least 1 hour so that the flavors have time to meld.

Lay the bread slices on a work surface. Using a serrated knife, cut off the crusts from each slice. Cut each slice into four 2-inch squares, or use a heart-shaped cookie cutter to make heart shapes. Spread 16 of the slices with the cheese mixture, dividing it evenly. Top with the remaining 16 slices and press firmly. Arrange the sandwiches on a serving platter. Garnish with the lemon thyme and serve.

Recipe continues on following page.

Continued from previous page.

PIMENTO CHEESE

4 oz cream cheese, softened

4 oz mild Cheddar cheese, shredded

2 tablespoons mayonnaise

1 tablespoon chopped canned
   pimentos

¼ teaspoon sea salt

¼ teaspoon black pepper

8 thin slices marble rye or other
   dark bread

2 fresh lemon-thyme sprigs,
   for garnish

SPICY CRAB SALAD

8 oz fresh crab meat

½ cup mayonnaise

1 tablespoon finely chopped green
   onions, green and white parts

1 tablespoon finely diced celery

2 tablespoons fresh lemon juice

½ tablespoon paprika, plus more
   for garnish

16 thin slices sourdough or other
   white bread

1 tablespoon chopped fresh dill,
   for garnish

1 lemon, sliced with peel, for garnish

To make the crab sandwiches, in a large bowl, combine the crab meat, mayonnaise, green onions, celery, lemon juice, and paprika. Place the crab mixture in the refrigerator for at least 1 hour so that the flavors have time to meld.

Lay the bread slices on a work surface. Using a serrated knife, cut off the crusts from each slice. Cut each slice into two 2-inch rectangles, or use a heart-shaped cookie cutter to make heart shapes. Spread 16 of the slices with the crab mixture, dividing it evenly. Top with the remaining 16 slices and press firmly. Arrange the sandwiches on a serving platter. Sprinkle paprika and the dill on top of the sandwiches and serve. For a garnish, place the lemon slices on the serving dish alongside the sandwiches.

COUNTESS: Look, here comes that
vulgar Brown woman.

RUTH: Quickly, get up before she sits with us.

(MOLLY BROWN WALKS UP, GREETING THEM
CHEERFULLY AS THEY ARE RISING.)

MOLLY: Hello girls, I was hoping I'd catch you at tea.

RUTH: We're awfully sorry you missed it.
The Countess and I are just off to
take the air on the boat deck.

MOLLY: What a lovely idea. I need to
catch up on the gossip.

"What? You think a first-class girl can't drink?"

—ROSE

COCKTAILS

 # OLD FASHIONED

The old fashioned cocktail is one of the oldest cocktails in the world. When the *Titanic* sailed, old fashioned cocktails had already been popular for many years, especially in Wisconsin, where Jack Dawson grew up. They can be made with whiskey or—for a sweeter adaptation—brandy. The garnish for the old fashioned sweet cocktail rarely, if ever, departs from the classic: a maraschino or brandied cherry and a twist of fresh orange.

MAKES 1 COCKTAIL

2 orange twists

6 dashes ginger bitters

½ teaspoon sugar

1 fl oz brandy

1 tablespoon water

1 cup lemon-lime soda

1 slice orange, for garnish

1 maraschino or brandied cherry,
   for garnish

Using a cocktail stirrer, muddle the orange twists, ginger bitters and sugar in a mixing glass. Add the brandy and water and stir until well chilled, 20–30 seconds. Pour into a highball glass filled with ice. Add the soda and stir. Garnish with the orange slice and cherry pieced together with a cocktail pick.

TRIVIA

There were more than 1,000 bottles of wine, 850 bottles of spirits, 191 liquor cases (850 bottles), and 20,000 bottles of beer listed on the *Titanic*'s manifest. Bottles of Champagne—including some marked "Heidsieck & Co" and some with "Deinhard & Co Coblenz" marked on the base of their cork—were found intact at the resting site of the *Titanic*. At least eight still contained Champagne. There were also bottles of Bordeaux, Burgundy, and fortified wines.

BRANDY SMASH

When Rose explains to her family that Jack saved her from falling overboard, Colonel Archibald Gracie says, "Well, the boy's a hero then! Good for you, son. Well done. So it's all's well and back to our brandy, eh?" Even in the scene just minutes before the *Titanic* sinks, passengers are still asking for brandy. Smash cocktails—made with fruit, herbs, or other ingredients muddled together—are often mixed with brandy or whiskey and served over crushed ice. Mint juleps and other smash cocktails were popularized throughout the 1800s among high-society circles in Virginia and Washington, DC. They would have been the favorite drinks of many first-class *Titanic* passengers. In this cocktail, brandy replaces whiskey for a lighter, brighter variation of a traditional whiskey mint julep. Pineapple mint provides a subtler, more complex flavor profile.

MAKES 1 COCKTAIL

3 leaves fresh pineapple mint

½ teaspoon sugar

1 cup lemon-lime soda

1 fl oz brandy

1 orange twist, for garnish

1 maraschino or brandied cherry,
   for garnish

2 fresh pineapple mint sprigs,
   for garnish

Using a muddler, muddle the pineapple mint and sugar in a cocktail glass. Add crushed ice to the glass. Add the soda and brandy and stir until well chilled, 20–30 seconds. Garnish with the orange twist, cherry, and pineapple mint.

"We are dressed in our best and are prepared to go down as gentlemen. But we would like a brandy!"

—MR. GUGGENHEIM

BLUE MOON

This cocktail showcases spring flowers that were in bloom when the *Titanic* sailed, including edible blooms like pansies and spring violets. Violet Jessop, one of the many brave young people aboard, was a stewardess who remarkably survived the sinkings of both the *Titanic* in 1912 and the *Britannic* in 1916. In 1911, several months before joining the staff of the *Titanic*, she also survived the crash and near-sinking of the *Olympic*. Violet told reporters that, on the last night on the *Titanic*, she bumped into *Titanic* first violinist John "Jock" Hume in the stairwell. He told her that the band was going to play songs to lift the spirits of passengers and crew members.

Crème de violette was popular—sipped on its own or with vermouth—as far back as the 1800s. It is the main ingredient in the classic blue moon cocktail, which became the signature cocktail at Joel's bar, located around the corner from Times Square when the *Titanic* sailed. This cocktail recipe is dedicated to the many young crew members aboard the *Titanic*, and especially the two courageous and inspiring friends Violet and Jock.

MAKES 1 COCKTAIL

2 fl oz gin

½ fl oz crème de violette

½ fl oz fresh lemon juice

1 lemon twist, for garnish

1 edible spring blossom, such as
   violet or pansy, for garnish

Combine the gin, crème de violette, and lemon juice in a mixing glass filled with ice. Stir until well chilled, 20–30 seconds. Strain into chilled coupe glass. Garnish with the lemon twist and spring blossom.

> MUSICIAN: What's the use?
> Nobody's listening to
> us anyway.
>
> WALLACE HARTLEY:
> Well, they don't listen to
> us at dinner either.

CITRUS BRONX

On a Sunday in 1906, bartender Johnny Solon visited the Bronx Zoo. A few days later, while he was working the lunch rush at the bar of first-class *Titanic* passenger John Jacob Astor IV's Waldorf-Astoria, a head waiter cajoled Solon into creating something new for an important patron. Solon had built a reputation for making mint juleps—spending 30 minutes making each one—and he embraced this new challenge. Solon looked around for ingredients to revamp the duplex cocktail, a mix of sweet and dry vermouth with bitters. He spied an orange, and he quickly coined a new gin recipe. "Better have plenty of oranges ordered for this one!" was the happy reaction from the lunch crowd. For a 1932 newspaper story titled "Fame Undying," Solon said: "I had been to the Bronx Zoo the Sunday before, and I had heard fellas talk of all the animals you'd see if you mixed drinks. So I calls it the Bronx!" In a nod to the *Titanic*'s destination, New York, the cocktail's blood orange enhances the citrusy flavor of Solon's legendary drink.

MAKES 1 COCKTAIL

1 fl oz gin

½ fl oz sweet vermouth

½ fl oz dry vermouth

1 fl oz fresh orange juice

4 dashes orange bitters

Juice of 1 blood orange

1 blood orange slice, for garnish

Combine the gin, vermouths, orange juice, and bitters in a mixing glass filled with ice. Stir for 20–30 seconds, then strain into a chilled coupe glass. Add the blood orange juice. Garnish with the blood orange slice.

FABRIZIO: [STANDING WITH JACK ON THE BOW] I can see the Statue of Liberty already...very small, of course!

TRIVIA

In the September 21, 1911 issue of the *St. Louis Post-Dispatch*, a cartoon featuring the famous "Weather Bird" points out that as the Bronx cocktail's popularity was growing, so was frustration over dry Sundays. The cartoon reads: "Why not let hotels sell Bronx cocktails on Sundays?" The *Post-Dispatch* called the Bronx cocktail "the golden dream of alcoholic delight" and wrote that "experts say five of 'em are a plenty."

ROB ROY

Although head baker Charles Joughin told his family that it was not whiskey, but schnapps, that he was drinking after the *Titanic* struck the iceberg, this recipe for a Rob Roy cocktail features the Scotch whiskey that Charles was thought to have been drinking. It is believed that the Rob Roy originated in 1894 at first-class *Titanic* passenger John Jacob Astor IV's Waldorf-Astoria hotel in New York. At the time, an operetta was being performed in town that told the story of a man who was considered a Scottish Robin Hood—Rob Roy MacGregor.

MAKES I COCKTAIL

2 fl oz blended Scotch whiskey

1 fl oz sweet vermouth

2 dashes cocoa bitters

2 chocolate mint leaves, finely chopped

1 maraschino or brandied cherry, for garnish

1 chocolate mint leaf, for garnish

Combine the whiskey, vermouth, cocoa bitters, and chocolate mint in a mixing glass filled with ice and stir until well chilled, 20–30 seconds. Strain into a chilled coupe glass. Garnish with the cherry and chocolate mint pieced together with a cocktail pick.

TRIVIA

There were chocolate cocktails around the time that the *Titanic* sailed. Less than two years after the *Titanic* sank, the *New York Times* reported that a man named Bud Weeks spotted two brown squirrels stumbling after digging into a box that had fallen off a truck near Tarrytown, New York. As Weeks got closer to the box and the squirrels struggled up a tree to their hole, he saw that the box was marked "Chocolate Cocktails." "They were just like a drunken man trying to put a key in a keyhole and had about as much success," Weeks said of the squirrels.

CLOVER CLUB

Developed by Philadelphia's Bellevue-Stratford Hotel on South Broad Street, this frothy and delicate drink is named for a local men's club that met regularly at the hotel from the late 1800s to the early 1900s.

MAKES 1 COCKTAIL

RASPBERRY-GERANIUM SYRUP

1 cup sugar

1 cup water

1 pint raspberries

1 large scented geranium leaf, finely chopped

COCKTAIL

1 fl oz fresh lemon juice

1 fl oz gin

1 fl oz dry vermouth

½ fl oz egg white (about ½ egg white)

1 lemon twist, for garnish

1 large scented geranium leaf, for garnish

To make the raspberry-geranium syrup, in a small saucepan over medium heat, combine the sugar and the water, stirring to dissolve the sugar. Reduce the heat to low, add the raspberries and geranium leaf, and simmer until the raspberries break down and the mixture reduces, 20–25 minutes. Remove from the heat and let cool to room temperature. Strain the syrup through a fine-mesh sieve set over a small jam or Mason jar. You should have about 1 cup of syrup.

To make the cocktail, combine the lemon juice, gin, vermouth, egg white, and 1 fl oz of the raspberry-geranium syrup in a cocktail shaker, cover, and shake until the egg white froths up and emulsifies, 10–15 seconds. Fill the shaker with ice, cover, and shake hard for about 10 seconds longer. Strain into a chilled coupe glass. Garnish with the lemon twist and germanium leaf.

> ENTERTAINING TIP: Bring your flavor profile full-circle by wrapping up your party with the flavors you started with. You can drizzle some of the leftover raspberry syrup over the Brownies (page 95) or the Honey Crêpes (page 74).

HORSE'S NECK

A 1910s twist on an 1890s mocktail, the horse's neck was a popular cocktail in New York before Prohibition. In the years just before the *Titanic* sailed, it became fashionable for bartenders to give the horse's neck some kick with whiskey or brandy. Whiskey gives the drink a little more punch, which in this recipe, is tempered nicely with a touch of peach nectar. With or without alcohol, this drink usually sports a long curly lemon zest garnish that inspired its name.

MAKES I COCKTAIL

1 fl oz Scotch whiskey

1 cup ginger ale

2 fl oz peach nectar

2 dashes angostura bitters

1 extra-long strip lemon zest,
   for garnish (see Tip)

1 thin peach slice, for garnish

Mix together the whiskey, ginger ale, peach nectar, and bitters in a Tom Collins glass filled with ice. Stir until well chilled, 20–30 seconds. Place the lemon zest inside the glass, with about one-third of it draping slightly over the side, and garnish with the peach slice.

COOK'S TIP: To make a decorative lemon zest "horse's neck" garnish, hold a medium lemon at the base. Using a small, sharp knife, start at the top and cut a ¼-inch-wide strip of peel around the lemon to make a spiral-shaped strip. Continue cutting the peel to the bottom of the lemon. Gently stretch out the peel and trim any fraying off the edges of both sides of the strip. Curl the peel back into a spiral and place it inside the glass, leaving about one-third of the peel draped slightly over the side of the glass.

ROBERT BURNS WITH LAVENDER SHORTBREAD COOKIES

This was a popular pre-Prohibition drink, according to Albert Stevens Crockett, author of *The Old Waldorf-Astoria Bar Book* (1934). "It may have been named after the celebrated Scotsman [Robert Burns]," he writes. "Chances are, however, that it was christened in honor of a cigar salesman, who 'bought' in the Old Bar." In *The Waldorf Astoria Bar Book* (2016), author Frank Caiafa writes a variation using Bénédictine that is clearly inspired by the Scottish poet, who lived in Dumfries, Scotland—coincidentally, where the *Titanic's* first violinist John "Jock" Hume lived about a century later. This version swaps the traditional dash of absinthe and orange bitters for lavender bitters and a shortbread cookie garnish.

MAKES 1 COCKTAIL; 12 COOKIES

LAVENDER SHORTBREAD

1 cup (2 sticks) unsalted butter, plus more for the pan

1 cup sugar

1 teaspoon pure vanilla extract

2 cups all-purpose flour

½ teaspoon salt

2 tablespoons lavender buds

2 cups chopped pecans or walnuts (optional)

ROBERT BURNS

2 fl oz blended Scotch whiskey

1 fl oz sweet vermouth

5 dashes lavender bitters

1 strip lemon peel

1 fresh lavender sprig

3 shortbread cookies

To make the lavender shortbread, preheat the oven to 325°F. Butter a baking sheet.

In a large bowl using a handheld mixer on medium-high speed, cream together the butter, sugar, and vanilla until well combined. While beating, gradually add the flour and salt. Continue to beat until the mixture is fluffy and light. Using your hands, mix the lavender buds and the pecans, if using, into the dough until thoroughly combined.

Using your hands, shape the dough into 1-inch balls. Place the balls evenly apart on the prepared baking sheet. Use the palm of your hand to press down each ball slightly.

Bake the cookies until the edges become lightly browned, 20–25 minutes. Remove the cookies and transfer them to a cooling rack.

While the cookies cool, make the cocktail. Combine the whiskey, vermouth, and lavender bitters in a mixing glass filled with ice and stir until well chilled, 20–30 seconds. Strain into a chilled coupe glass. Garnish with the lemon peel and lavender and serve next to 3 small shortbread cookies on a small plate.

> ENTERTAINING TIP: Host your *Titanic* party on Burns Night, which is celebrated each year on January 25. The special day acknowledges the contributions of Scottish poet Robert Burns. Traditional suppers on Burns Night include Cullen skink (fish soup made with haddock); haggis (English-style pudding made with offals); and neeps and tatties (mashed potatoes and turnips).

BIBLIOGRAPHY

BOOKS & ARTICLES

Bain, Zoe. "Titanic Final Lunch Menu to Sell for More Than $150,000." Delish. February 28, 2012.

Bandurski, Katie. "12 Amazing Foods People Ate Aboard the Titanic." *Readers Digest.* July 2021.

Brandeis, Erich. "Looking at Life." *Standard Sentinel.* November 14, 1936.

Broad Ax. December 9, 1905.

Brownstone, Cecily. "Peach melba fans never had it so good." *Index Journal.* March 19, 1962.

Carew, Kate. "Dr. Cook tells Kate Carew about gumdrops." *San Francisco Examiner.* January 15, 1911.

Cloake, Felicity. "How to make Eton Mess." *Guardian.* August 15, 2018.

Delano, Edith Barnard. "Setting The Table." *Meriden Daily Journal.* November 15, 1911.

"Fame undying." *Ironwood Daily Globe.* July 13, 1932.

"Fancy China and bric-a-brac are greatly reduced in price." *Sandusky Register.* December 12, 1911.

"Free demonstration, Borden's malted milk, P. Wiest's Sons." *York Dispatch.* September 22, 1904.

Glasgow Herald. October 13, 1892.

"Gougeres: French pastries add to summer meal." *Beckley Post Herald.* July 11, 1975.

Hebert, Malcolm, R. "Vive le Calfouti!" *Fort Lauderdale News,* September 20, 1987.

"Here's the recipe for the first-ever Brownie, Invented in Chicago: It was served by the Palmer House at the World's Columbian Exposition of 1893." *Chicago Magazine.* October 12, 2016.

"History of Plum Puddings." *York Daily.* March 14, 1891.

"Items from luxury liner sell for thousands." Associated Press. May 14, 1999.

Jones, Alfred, C. "Dallas resident recalls *Titanic. Capital Journal.* April 15, 1972.

Kansas City Star. July 15, 1910.

"Make mine a malted milk." *Quad City Times.* June 4, 1915.

Monroe, Lilla Day. "The lunch basket." *Topeka Daily Capital.* June 25, 1911.

Moran, Lee. "Rare menu from Titanic's second class restaurant to be auctioned for $135G." *New York Daily News.* April 22, 2014.

Morriarty, Gerry. "Last lunch menu for 'Titanic' first-class passengers goes on display in Belfast." *Irish Times*. March 22, 2013.

"Old Maid Party." *Daily Democrat*. October 14, 1905.

"One of silk mill owners was on *Titanic*." *Daily New Era*. April 18, 1912.

Richard, Jackie. "Presenting the…asparagus." *San Bernardino Sun*.

Robinson, Julian. "Pea soup, grilled mutton chops and cheese to follow (but the Welsh rarebit was off): Lunch menu from the Titanic just two days before disaster set to sell for $110,000." *Daily Mail*. October 9, 2014.

Rubin, Daniel. "Local survivors of the Titanic recall the horror." *Philadelphia Inquirer*. December 19, 1997.

Schumann, Marguerite. "Former Laurentian's cookbook features Molly Brown recipes." *Post-Crescent*. April 30, 1967.

Shaw, David. "Still looking for love in L.A." *Los Angeles Times*. May 12, 2005.

"Silence Cloth." *Cody Cowboy*. April 21, 1911.

"Squirrels were drunk: Chocolate cocktails they found sent them home staggering." *New York Times*. January 26, 1914.

Standard. October 25, 1892.

Steinkopf, Alvin. "Tiddlywinks game snapping back in Britain." Associated Press, London. *Daily Reporter*. July 3, 1958.

Sun. August 6, 1911.

"The car that went down with the Titanic." Fox News. October 10, 2016.

"The most popular indoor games are Flinch and Bourse." *York Dispatch*. September 22, 1904.

"The true story of Eton Mess – and how to make the perfect one." *Country Life*. June 22, 2019.

"Used gumdrops to find pole: Eskimos fond of the chewy confection——Used as reward for extra efforts." *Morning Register*. September 26, 1909.

"Utensils provide interesting lesson in world history." *Daily Herald*. November 16, 1997.

Vermeulen, Michael. "Everyone homes in on the 'priiize.'" *Chicago Daily News*. September 25, 1977.

Wallace, Elizabeth Victoria. *Hidden History of Denver*. The History Press, 2011.

Ward, Christopher. *And The Band Played On*. Hodder & Stoughton. 2012.

Westminster Budget. May 11, 1894.

"Whole family safe from Titanic wreck. *Brooklyn Daily Eagle*. April 18, 1912.

"Why not let hotels sell Bronx cocktails on Sundays?" Weather Bird cartoon. *St. Louis Post-Dispatch*. September 21, 1911.

Will-Weber, Mark. *Mint Juleps with Teddy Roosevelt*. Regnery History, 2014.

Wondrich, David. "History Lesson: The Blue Moon Cocktail." *Imbibe*. April 11, 2013.

Wright, Terry. "Titanic anniversary interests Flemington attorney Louis Miller." *Hunterdon County Democrat*. March 30, 2019.

BLOGS & WEBSITES

"An Edwardian Dinner Party." January 8, 2013. *Brighton Museum: https://brightonmuseums.org.uk/.*

"An Extremely Rare Original Titanic 3rd Class Menu Postcard, 14th April 1912." May 1, 2005. *Bonhams: https://www.bonhams.com/.*

"Classic Hershey Candy: WHOPPERS Malted Milk Balls." *Hersheyland: https://hersheyland.com.*

"Did John Bartram introduce rhubarb to North America? Joel Fry, Curator at Bartram's Garden, answers the question…." July 12, 2012. *Growing History: https://growinghistory.wordpress.com/2012/07/20/did-john-bartram-introduce-rhubarb-to-north-america/.*

"Dining and Dinners." January 28, 2010. *https://Edwardian Promenade: www.edwardianpromenade.com/etiquette/dining-and-dinners/.*

Doyle, Michelle. "Afternoon Tea at The V&A. October 29, 2018. *The V&A: https://www.vam.ac.uk/.*

Feather, Lauren. "Deep Dish Vs. NYC Style: Which City Offers A Better Slice?" February 24, 2022. *The Travel: https://www.thetravel.com/.*

"History of Afternoon Tea." *Lady Bedford: http://ladybedfords.com.*

"Object History: Horlick's Malted Milk." Wisconsin 101. Our History in Objects. September 9, 2020. *Wisconsin 101: https://wi101.wisc.edu/horlicks-malted-milk-company/.*

"Second Class dinner menu from the last night on the RMS 'Titanic,' 14 April, 1912, kept by survivor Mrs. Bertha J. Marshall (nee Watt)." *Royal Museum Greenwich: https://prints.rmg.co.uk.*

Tamzilo, Bobby. "Jeffers will convert former Horlick Malted Milk Plant into town center." June 25, 2020. *OnMilwauke: https://onmilwaukee.com/.*

"The Great Escoffier and The Appeal of The French Chef." *East Riding Museums: https://www.eastridingmuseums.co.uk/.*

"The Manners of The Edwardian Era." May 16, 2016. *Driehouse Museum: https://driehausmuseum.org/.*

"Titanic bandsmen as documented by survivors." July 27, 2012 *Titanic Piano Blog: https://titanicpiano.blog/2012/07/27/titanics-bandsmen-as-documented-by-survivors/.*

"Titanic Tea." *Belle Grove Plantation: https://www.bellegroveplantation.com/calendar/titanic-tea.*

"Victorian Gloves: Etiquette for Use." *Recollections: https://recollections.biz/blog/victorian-gloves-etiquette-for-use/.*

www.Encyclopedia-Titanica.org.

INDEX

INSIGHT
EDITIONS

PO Box 3088
San Rafael, CA 94912
www.insighteditions.com

A WELDON OWEN PRODUCTION

CEO Raoul Goff
VP Publisher Roger Shaw
Associate Publisher Amy Marr
Editorial Director Katie Killebrew
Assistant Editor Jourdan Plautz
Editorial Assistant Kayla Belser
VP Creative Chrissy Kwasnik
Art Director Allister Fein
Designer Leah Bloise Lauer
Sr Production Manager Joshua Smith
Sr Production Manager, Subsidiary Rights Lina s Palma-Temena

Photography Waterbury Publications, Des Moines, IA
Food Stylist Jennifer Peterson
Weldon Owen would also like to thank Lesley Bruynesteyn.

ISBN: 978-1-64722-857-6

Manufactured in China by Insight Editions

10 9 8 7 6 5 4 3 2

ROOTS of PEACE   ⊕ REPLANTED PAPER

Insight Editions, in association with Roots of Peace, will plant two trees for each tree used in the manufacturing of
this book. Roots of Peace is an internationally renowned humanitarian organization dedicated to eradicating land
mines worldwide and converting war-torn lands into productive farms and wildlife habitats. Roots of Peace will plant
two million fruit and nut trees in Afghanistan and provide farmers there with the skills and support necessary for
sustainable land use.